THE ACID REFLUX COOKBOOK

1200 Days of Tasty and Healthy Recipes to Quickly Reduce Symptoms of GERD & LPR A 28-Day Stress-Free Meal Plan for Heartburn Relief

Harriett Noris

TABLE OF CONTENTS

INTRODUCTION

The human body is complex – it is a machine crafted very well. Everything is connected, and all the organs and tissues are perfectly synchronized. If one thing goes wrong, it will also directly affect the rest of the body.

Our stomach is one of the integral organs of the body that affects many other parts. If your stomach is not working as it should, your skin will be dull, and you will have acne, scars, heartburn, bloating, pain, and a feeling of unrest. Among all these things, you may feel acid reflux.

Acid reflux is a condition of having a burning pain that is similar to heartburn in the lower chest, food pipe, or throat. When the stomach acid flows upward to the food pipe, it causes an acidic feeling in the pipe and lower chest. Sometimes in severe conditions, it can come up to the throat, causing severe pain and unease.

Acid reflux seems common – some may experience it daily, once a week, or every 15 to 20 days. A person is diagnosed with gastric acid reflux when they experience the feeling more than twice a week. In such conditions, the person must move forward and ask for medical help.

CHAPTER 1:
Causes and Symptoms of Acid Reflux

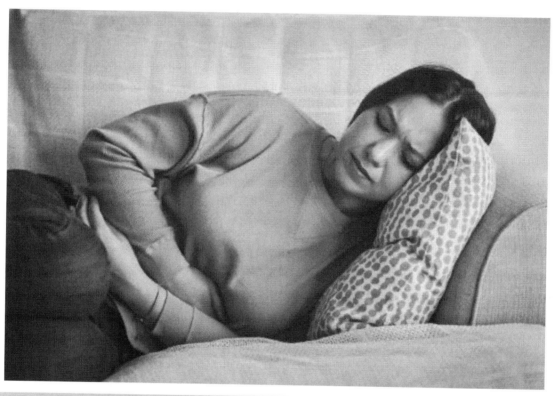

Causes of Acid Reflux

Before heading to a doctor, it is necessary to look into the causes of acid reflux. Whenever our body is not functioning properly, or an organ behaves differently, there are certain reasons behind that. It is essential to identify these reasons and problems in the first place. When you know the causes, you can move toward a better treatment and prevention system. Therefore, here we are, discussing some of the major causes of acid reflux.

Hiatus or Hernia

One of the non-preventable causes of acid reflux is the Hiatus or Hernia. It is a condition when a hole in the diaphragm leads to the stomach's upper part entering the chest cavity. This situation can cause the acid from the stomach to reflux in the upper canal and cause a burning sensation in the throat and chest section.

It is one of the critical conditions in overall human health, as the person will not be able to control the factor. Only surgery and proper hernia treatment can help avoid gastric acid reflux in such conditions. There is a 100% chance of acid reflux in hernia patients, as both sections intersect in this situation.

Obesity

Another cause of gastric acid reflux is obesity. When there is a lack of weight management, our body behaves differently. Weight that is above average has an intense reaction in the body. Organs start behaving differently, which can result in issues. Obesity is not normal; it is connected to several health risks. Increased weight and mass affect total body stamina, bone strength, heart performance, blood circulation, hormonal changes, and organ activities.

Gastric acid reflux is one of the significant outcomes that are related to obesity. The stomach cannot digest all the food properly, and the acid release is an effort to deal with the excessive energy left in the body. It causes the outward flow of acid from the stomach. Moreover, obesity can affect the stomach size, and its movement can trigger the condition of acid reflux.

Smoking

Smoking is one of the biggest causes of acid reflux. It is known that cigarettes and cigars have acidic reactions in the body. Smoking affects the overall organ system composition as well. It can affect not only the lungs but the stomach. In response to the smoke and all the chemicals in it, the acid in the stomach reaches the food canal in reverse. When the person inhales and exhales smoke, it can come up with fumes of acid from the stomach, increasing the risks and effects of gastric acid reflux.

Alcohol

Another major cause of acid reflux is the use of alcohol. Alcoholism is dangerous for a person's overall health. It affects the lifestyle and internal organs of the body. The consumption of alcohol is good if kept within a safe limit, but when there is excessive use, there will be problems. Acid reflux is one of the problems that are caused as a result of excessive alcohol consumption. The important thing is to keep the consumption of alcohol in a routine and keep it limited for safe use.

No or Low Physical Activity

Our food is digested in our stomach, and two major things trigger the process. One is acid, and the other is physical activity. If a person eats and has no or low physical activity, there can be a chance of acid reflux. The stomach will produce acid to digest food, but the excessive amount of acid will produce reflux in the food canal in the event of no activity. It is vital to have a walk after a meal or exert your body physically to trigger the proper digestion of your food. It will help you make things better and smoother. Physical activity will help you better use acid in the stomach and dissolve it in the food. It will neutralize the acid in the digestion process and will get you all the necessary nutrients you need.

Multiple Drugs and Sedatives

Sometimes the sedative medications and anti-depressant drugs we take can cause acidity in the stomach. That acidity can lead to ultimate gastric acid reflux. It is necessary to have a safe and limited dosage of the drugs. The excessive use of medicine, especially without prescriptions, could affect your overall stomach functions.

Pregnancy

During pregnancy, numerous changes occur. Everything changes, from mood swings to food options and psychological ideas to physical movements. During this process, females face threats, many of which are critical health constraints. It can sometimes happen due to a lack of care, vitamins, or excessive use of a specific product. There are occasionally genetic reactions in the body as well. Acid reflux is not inherited but can be caused by pregnancy and body changes. Your stomach may behave differently, and you may not get as much physical movement, leading to a reflux situation.

Moreover, the vomiting and constant nausea caused by pregnancy can always trigger gastric acid reflux. In this regard, the important thing is to monitor everything and then have essential solutions.

Poor Dietary Selection

Your food intake and dietary choices matter a lot when it comes to your overall health. Poor dietary options can trigger acid reflux. You may suffer from acid reflux if you consume junk food, soft drinks, dried snacks, and fat-rich food options. Such food options increase the acidity in the stomach and can result in issues.

Improper Posture After Meal

Medical deficiencies and complications do not just cause acid reflux. It can come up as a reaction to bad posture. It is necessary to ensure proper physical posture when having a meal. Bending over your waist or lying on your back while eating or right after taking a meal can result in acid reflux. It can be dangerous and build up the issue for more serious causes. It is necessary to watch out during your meal and pay attention to your movement routine to avoid such drastic outcomes from your activities.

Bedtime Snacks

Bedtime snacking is one of the everyday habits that people have. It is a kind of routine for people in many cases. On the other hand, it is one of the critical causes of acid reflux. Eating food at bedtime does not allow it to digest properly, and the physical posture that often accompanies bedtime snacking can cause the stomach acids to reflux upwards.

Symptoms of Acid Reflux

Most people confuse gastric acid reflux with heartburn. Sometimes it is claimed that both are the same, and sometimes, they are marked as different. Although there is an acceptable difference between the two, it is necessary to underline this by focusing on the symptoms of acid reflux. You can fight a medical condition after knowing its causes and major symptoms. The symptoms are necessary for better evaluation and diagnosis.

Acid reflux is one of the conditions that people do not take seriously in the beginning. They only become concerned when things get a bit out of control. To live healthily, the important thing is to keep the symptoms and all changes in the body under consideration. It is good to know the major symptoms and take note of these symptoms. Eventually, it will help in self and early diagnosis, and you can come up with the best remedies and treatments. Here are a few major symptoms of gastric acid reflux to consider:

- Heartburn is one of the major symptoms of acid reflux. It is not the same thing, but the first step that leads to the condition. You can feel discomfort or pain with a burning sensation in your abdomen and chest area that goes up to your throat.
- Bitter tasting in the back of the mouth and throat is another symptom that shows bad stomach conditions and acid reflux.
- A burning sensation in the upper throat can be a reaction to acid reflux.
- The feeling of nausea or wanting to throw up the food you just had.
- Continuous burping with a bad smell and acidic feeling.
- Vomit can be bloody and painful in severe cases.
- Acid reflux can cause black and bloody stools, accompanied by a burning sensation.
- There can be difficult hiccups with a mixed feeling of pain and burning.
- The immense reduction in weight can be observed without any reason.
- Sore throat, dry cough, and wheezing can occur in the initial and chronic stages of acid reflux.
- There can be a feeling of unease in the throat like food is stuck in the throat.
- Difficulty in swallowing food, accompanied by the feeling of pain and burning.
- Bad breath and dental erosion are other major symptoms of acid reflux.

The condition of acid reflux not only affects the stomach and causes a burning sensation inside. It leads to some major outcomes. If there is no proper treatment for the condition, then the results can be drastic. It can start as a simple problem of indigestion or acidity in the stomach that will lead to burping and even end up resulting in bloody vomit, difficulty swallowing, and much more. Identifying these basic symptoms is necessary, as measures must be taken to resolve these issues quickly.

You can get to know more symptoms of acid reflux in some instances. Everyone doesn't necessarily face the same issues in the beginning. The person could have any of these or all of these symptoms from time to time. The best way is to be alert with the treatment, even if you face initial or minor symptoms. Sometimes you may have these issues mixed with any other health condition. During these times, immediately make sure to discuss this with your personal doctor.

Remember, bad smell and throat issues largely come from your stomach; if these go unnoticed, you may have to face the music. Note the symptoms and related signs of the problem and consider these things in your daily routine for early diagnosis and control of the problem.

CHAPTER 2:
Foods To Avoid and Foods To Eat

What To Eat

The foods below will help you manage the symptoms of acid reflux. When you feel acid reflux, try to eat one or some of these foods to help you. Some may work better for you than others, so don't get discouraged if you eat something and don't feel a huge difference. Eventually, you will find the foods that work best for you.

Vegetables

We all know that vegetables are good for us. If anything, adding more vegetables to your diet will increase the number of nutrients your body is getting. They are naturally low in fat and acid. Some good options are leafy green vegetables, potatoes, cucumber, broccoli, and cauliflower.

Ginger

Please don't think you must chomp down on a whole thumb of ginger. Thankfully, you do not need a lot of it to gain its benefits. Adding sliced or crushed pieces to your food or smoothies is a great way to incorporate ginger into your diet. You could also make ginger tea. Ginger is a natural anti-inflammatory food and is particularly good for many gastrointestinal problems.

Oats

Anything high in fiber benefits your digestive system and can help relieve acid reflux. Oats are easy to make and have a lot of fiber in them. You can easily incorporate it into your diet by having it for breakfast with fruit.

Non-Citrus Fruit

Fruit is generally exceptionally good for you, so you will do your body good if you increase the amount you eat. Citrus is high in acid, so you should avoid those types of fruit. Some of the fruit that you can incorporate into your diet are bananas, apples, melons, and pears.

Lean Meat and Seafood

The key word here is lean. These types of meats are low in fat and high in protein. Some examples of these foods are seafood, turkey, and chicken. Cooking them by grilling, poaching, and baking is best. Always avoid frying.

Egg Whites

The entire egg is filled with nutrients and protein, but the yolk is also high in fat. This could trigger acid reflux. Sticking to the whites is a great way to get in the protein without the added fat.

Healthy Fats

Good fats can help with acid reflux. It is the saturated and trans fats that cause a significant problem. While eating large amounts of fat is not good, healthy fats are packed full of nutrients and can help lessen the symptoms of acid reflux. Sources of healthy fats include avocados, nuts, flaxseed, and olive oil.

What To Avoid

There has been some debate about what food causes acid reflux. However, certain foods have been shown to cause acid problems in many people. You may have noticed that you get heartburn when you eat a certain food. While food might not be the only cause of acid reflux, it can be a trigger. Avoiding anything that could make your body unhappy is key to controlling the symptoms. Take a look at this list of common trigger foods and see if there is anything you have experienced problems with.

Fatty Foods

This is a broad category, but I'm sure there were a few foods that popped into your mind when you read that. Fried foods, fast food, full-fat dairy, and fatty meats are all included. Fatty foods delay the stomach from emptying and cause stomach acid to back up. It is better to avoid these foods as much as you can. They generally cause more harm than good.

Citrus Fruit and Tomatoes

These are very acidic fruits and are unsuitable for people suffering from acid-related problems. Do your best to avoid them. Some of the fruit on the list are oranges, lemons, and pineapples.

Chocolate

This is a food that most people would be sad to avoid. Unfortunately, chocolate has been shown to increase acid reflux due to the presence of something called methylxanthine.

Spicy Food

These foods won't cause reflux in every person, but they can cause problems for some. It is best to track what happens to your body when you eat foods like this. Sometimes, the specific way it's cooked or the dish itself is the problem, not the whole food category.

Caffeine and Mint

Some people have been reported to suffer from acid reflux after having a cup of coffee or chewing on a piece of mint gum. If you notice this, then try and avoid these two things. Instead, go for caffeine-free coffee and mint-free gum and sweets.

What To Drink

We already know that drinks high in caffeine, highly acidic drinks, and carbonated drinks are not good for acid reflux. However, we haven't discussed the types of drinks you should consume. Do not overlook this. You should not drink too many liquids as this could cause acid reflux, but many drinks are good for you.

Herbal Teas

Herbal teas are great for aiding digestion and various digestive problems. Chamomile, licorice, and ginger teas are the best for acid reflux. They calm the stomach and can help soothe you. Just remember to avoid mint teas.

Smoothies

These are a great way to get added nutrients into your diet. The best part is that you can add ingredients that will help soothe your heartburn. Bananas, apples, ginger, and non-citrus fruits are all great options. Smoothies are easy to digest, easy to swallow, and very cool when they go down. A smoothie with the right ingredients can help with acid reflux and its symptoms.

Fruit Juices

We have already spoken about avoiding citrus fruits in your diet, but citrus fruits are not the only fruit that makes excellent juices. There are plenty of non-citrus fruits that can be juiced. One of the best ways to get your fruit juice is cold-pressed juices. These retain their nutrients and are free from unnecessary ingredients and flavorings. You can buy them in the shops or buy a juicer and juice your fruit and veggies. Some great options are carrot, ginger, aloe vera, watermelon, and cucumber.

Water

We should all be getting enough water into our diets. The PH of the water is neutral, which can help raise the PH of an acidic meal. Drinking too much water can adversely affect acid reflux, so don't overdo it. If you drink when you are thirsty, you should be fine. It is best not to overthink this one.

Food Swaps

Food swaps are one of the best ways to transition into a new diet or way of eating. We all have our favorites, and sometimes it can be hard to give certain things up. Food swapping allows you to use something similar in place of the food or ingredients you love. Let's look at some food swaps you can make daily.

Coffee for Herbal Tea

There are many coffee drinkers, but unfortunately, caffeine makes it bad for those who suffer from acid reflux. If you still want a nice warm drink, try going for herbal teas instead. They are much easier on the stomach and many teas aid in digestion. You can add some milk for a creamier drink if you are not happy with just tea and water.

Once you get used to drinking tea, you won't miss coffee. Just push through until you no longer crave coffee. Remember that caffeine is addictive, and that is why so many people struggle to give up coffee. If you have coffee multiple times a day, you might have to either wean yourself off it or suffer a few withdrawal symptoms before you can go without it. Don't be disheartened if it is a bit hard at the beginning. You will eventually not even miss it.

Citrus Fruit for Berries and Melons

The reason so many people love citrus fruit is that they are so juicy and sweet. Fortunately, there are plenty of other fruits that have the same characteristics. They may not taste the same, but melons and berries are juicy and delicious. Fill your fridge and fruit basket with these fruits instead of citrus fruits.

I would go as far as to say that berries and melons are much better than citrus fruits in terms of variety and usability. You can cook with berries much easier and transform them into your dishes. Using them as garnishes and toppings is also a great idea. Smoothies with these fruits are also super delicious. The possibilities are endless.

Chocolate for Carob Powder or Alkalized Cocoa

I think giving up chocolate is one that makes many people who suffer from acid reflux incredibly sad. Almost everyone enjoys a block of chocolate. The thing is, chocolate is both high in fat and acidic. That is a double trigger, which is why it is best just to give it a skip if you suffer from acid reflux. If you can have a block now and then without it triggering heartburn, then, by all means, go for it. Just be careful and don't overdo it.

Try carob powder or alkalized cocoa if you need a chocolate fix. Alkalized cocoa is also called Dutch-processed powder and is more alkaline than acidic. This makes it safe for people who suffer from acid reflux. Carob powder is not related to cocoa and comes from the carob pod. It has similar flavors to cocoa; you can use it in any recipe that asks for cocoa.

Now it is not a smart idea to just grab a spoonful of these powders and eat it straight. They will have a very bitter taste. You need to add them to the dishes. Chocolate cakes and desserts can be made using either of these, which should satisfy your chocolate craving.

Fried Food for Baked Food

Fried food is generally bad for everyone, even if they don't suffer from acid reflux. The high-fat content is a massive contributor to weight gain, and it is also a trigger for acid reflux. It is best to skip fried foods and try to cut them out of your diet as much as possible.

You can bake anything that you can fry. Since the cooking method is changing here, you don't have to change the actual foods you are eating. Plenty of recipes turn regular fried foods into healthy, baked alternatives. Some of these recipes are in the recipe section of this book so give them a try.

High Fat Dairy for Plant-Based Options

Dairy products are also a common acid reflux trigger. Again, this can be hard for people to give up since it seems almost to be a staple in everybody's home. The good news is that there are plenty of plant-based dairy alternatives. These are easy to get at supermarkets, and many are not too expensive.

Milk alternatives are soy milk, almond milk, and oat milk. Instead of regular yogurt, go for coconut yogurt. You can use all of these as direct substitutes for typical dairy products. So that makes it easy to add to your favorite recipes. You can get vegan cheese if you are looking for a cheese substitute. It is more expensive than regular cheese. But if you want a sprinkle of cheese, it is an option. You can also add a bit of nutritional yeast to your meal's cheesy flavor.

Tomato Pasta Sauce for Pesto

Tomato sauces on pasta are classic, but that is not the only way to enjoy pasta. Pesto is a great way to eat pasta, and it is delicious. You could also use some olive oil over your pasta for a simpler dish. Pasta is excellent with many things, so don't feel stuck because you give the red sauce a skip. You could also try making the low-acid tomato sauce recipe if you are craving some tomato paste. It is a great way to enjoy the red sauce still. Again, just be careful not to overdo it since not all the acid will be neutralized.

Garlic and Onions for Dried Versions

Although never eaten independently, these two add a lot of flavor to food. Many dishes require one or both, so it can be difficult to get a flavorful dish without them. Instead of using fresh garlic and onions, try the dried variety. They are less likely to cause acid reflux. The other bonus is that you don't always have to chop onions or crush garlic when making a meal.

There is a chance that the dried variety might still be a trigger for you. If this is the case, try using other herbs and spices for flavor. Basil, dill, and parsley add a lot of flavor to various dishes. None of them tastes like garlic or onion, but that does not mean you won't be able to get a delicious-tasting meal using them.

Alcohol for Non-Alcoholic Alternatives

Unfortunately, alcohol is a big acid reflux trigger, so it is best to avoid it altogether. If you are slightly tolerant, you can perhaps have one drink. However, be sure not to overdo it. It is important to know your limits as your health is the most important thing.

Thankfully, you have alcohol-free options if you enjoy having a drink on certain occasions. You should still avoid carbonated beverages, so it will not be a good idea to have non-alcoholic champagne and non-alcoholic beer. Instead, enjoy non-alcoholic wines and mocktails (which taste like regular cocktails without alcohol). In any case, you don't need alcohol in your life. It isn't a staple, so don't feel like you are missing out because you can't have a drink.

CHAPTER 3:
Breakfast

1. Muesli-Style Oatmeal

Preparation Time: 5 minutes

Cooking Time: 0 minutes

Servings: 1

Ingredients:

- 1 c. oatmeal
- 1 c. almond milk
- 2 tbsps. raisins
- 1 apple, peeled and diced
- A pinch of salt
- 2 tsp. Splenda

Directions:

- Soak oatmeal in milk, salt, Splenda, and raisins in a glass bowl.
- Cover and refrigerate the bowl for 2 hours.
- Stir in apples.
- Serve.

Nutrition:

Calories: 519

Total Fat: 31.4 g

Saturated Fat: 25.9 g

Cholesterol: 0 mg

Sodium: 99 mg

Total Carbs: 57.8 g

Fiber: 8.7 g

Sugar: 2.3 g

Protein: 6.5 g

2. Quinoa Porridge

Preparation Time: 5 minutes

Cooking Time: 15 minutes

Servings: 4

Ingredients:

- ¾ c. quinoa
- 3 c. almond milk
- 3 tbsps. Splenda
- ½ tsp. vanilla extract
- Salt to taste

Directions:

- Boil milk in a cooking pot and whisk in quinoa.
- Stir and cook the mixture until smooth and creamy.
- Add salt, vanilla, and Splenda.
- Serve.

Nutrition:

Calories: 544, Total Fat: 24.9 g , Saturated Fat: 4.7 g, Cholesterol: 194 mg , Sodium: 607 mg , Total Carbs: 30.7 g , Fiber: 1.4 g , Sugar: 3.3 g , Protein: 6.4g

3. Pear Banana Nut Muffins

Preparation Time: 5 minutes

Cooking Time: 25 minutes

Servings: 8

Ingredients:

- 1 medium pear, peeled and diced
- 2 tbsps. pear nectar
- 1 c. coconut flour
- 1 c. rolled oats
- 1 tbsp. ground flaxseed
- 3 tbsps. maple flakes
- 1 tsp. Baking powder
- ½ tsp. baking soda
- 1 tsp. Cinnamon
- ¼ tsp. Cardamom
- ¼ tsp. sea salt
- 2 egg whites
- ⅓ c. vanilla almond milk
- 2 tbsps. almond butter, melted
- 2 tsps. vanilla
- 1 medium banana, peeled and mashed
- 1 c. chopped walnuts

Directions:

- Set the oven to 375F. Layer a muffin tray with a paper liner and olive oil.
- Mix pear with pear nectar in a saucepan and boil it.
- Decrease the heat and cook for 3 minutes. Turn off the heat and allow it to cool.
- Mix flour with maple flakes, flaxseed, oats, baking soda, baking powder, salt, cinnamon, and cardamom in a bowl.
- Whisk pear mixture with almond milk, butter, vanilla, banana, and egg whites.
- Stir in the flour mixture and mix well.
- Fold in walnuts and mix well.
- Divide the mixture into the muffin tray.
- Bake for 20 minutes.
- Serve.

Nutrition: Calories: 408 , Total Fat: 16.5 g , Saturated Fat: 5 g , Cholesterol: 8 mg , Sodium: 285 mg , Total Carbs: 56.1 g , Fiber: 8.7 g , Sugar: 10.1 g , Protein: 11 g

4. Pumpkin Pancakes

Preparation Time: 5 minutes

Cooking Time: 20 minutes

Servings: 6

Ingredients:

- 2 c. coconut flour
- 2 tbsps. Splenda
- 1 tbsp. Splenda
- 2 tsps. baking powder
- 1 tsp. Baking soda
- ½ tsp. salt
- 1 c. pumpkin puree
- 1 tsp. Ground cinnamon
- ½ tsp. Ground ginger
- ½ tsp. ground allspice
- 1 egg white
- 1 ½ c. almond milk
- 2 tbsps. vegetable oil

Directions:

- Mix flour with sugar, baking powder, soda, salt, and Splenda in a large bowl.
- Combine pumpkin puree, ginger, cinnamon, allspice, egg whites, milk, and oil in another bowl.
- Stir in the flour mixture and mix well.
- Heat a greased skillet and pour a cup of batter into the pan.
- Cook for 3 minutes per side.
- Make more pancakes to use the entire batter.
- Serve.

Nutrition: Calories: 284 , Total Fat: 7.9 g , Saturated Fat: 0 g , Cholesterol: 36 mg , Sodium: 704 mg , Total Carbs: 46 g , Fiber: 3.6 g , Sugar: 5.5 g , Protein: 7.9 g

5. Coconut Rice Pudding

Preparation Time: 30 minutes

Cooking Time: 20 minutes

Servings: 4

Ingredients:

- ½ c. Coconut milk
- ¼ c. Milk
- ½ tsp. Ginger, ground
- 1 oz. Vanilla pudding mix
- ¼ c. Coconut, shredded
- 2 c. Brown rice, cooked
- 1 Pear, grated
- 2 tbsps. Honey
- ¼ c. Figs, dried

Directions:

- Bring out a pan and add the honey, coconut milk, milk, and pear on medium heat. Let this mixture get to a boil, and then take all of the ingredients from the heat.
- When this is done, slowly add the rice, ginger, coconut, and pudding mix to this pan.
- Mix it well, then set it to the side for a bit. It will take around ten minutes to finish this up and cool down.
- When that time is done, stir in the figs and mix them gently before serving and enjoying.

Nutrition:

Calories: 56

Total Fat: 4 g

Saturated Fat: 0.5 g

Fiber: 1.2 g

Sugar: 1 g

6. Pasta Salad

Preparation Time: 20 minutes

Cooking Time: 20 minutes

Servings: 6

Ingredients:

- 1 recipe of creamed herbed dressing
- ¼ c. Chopped basil
- ¼ c. Black olives, sliced
- ¼ c. Canned chickpeas
- 1 c. Baby spinach
- 2 c. Elbow macaroni

Directions:

- Take a big bowl and toss the basil, olives, chickpeas, spinach, and macaroni.
- When this is done, add some of the dressing, toss it around, and serve immediately.

Nutrition:

Calories: 120

Total Fat: 4 g

Saturated Fat: 0.5 g

Fiber: 1.2 g

Sugar: 1 g

7. Quick Banana Sorbet

Preparation Time: 5 minutes

Cooking Time: 0 minutes

Servings: 1

Ingredients:

- 3 bananas, peeled
- 1 tbsp. Ginger, peeled and grated finely
- ⅛ tsp. ground cardamom
- 2 tbsps. Honey
- ¼ tsp. salt
- 3 c. ice

Directions:

- Blend bananas with cardamom, salt, honey, and ginger in a blender.
- Stir in ice and blend again until smooth.
- Enjoy.

Nutrition:

Calories: 462

Total Fat: 1.5 g

Saturated Fat: 0.5 g

Cholesterol: 0 mg

Total Carbs: 119.8 g

Dietary Fiber: 10 g

Sugar: 78 g

Protein: 4.5 g

8. Oatmeal With Blueberries, Sunflower Seeds

Preparation Time: 10 minutes

Cooking Time: 25 minutes

Servings: 1

Ingredients:

- 1 serving of quick-cooking or old-fashioned rolled oats
- ½ c. blueberries
- 1 tbsp. sunflower seeds
- 1 tbsp. agave nectar

Directions:

- Cook oats as per the given instructions on the box.
- Add blueberries, sunflower seeds, and agave nectar.
- Serve.

Nutrition:

Calories: 134

Total Fat: 4.7 g

Saturated Fat: 0.6 g

Cholesterol: 0 mg

Sodium: 1 mg

Total Carbs: 54.1 g

Fiber: 7 g

Sugar: 23.3 g

Protein: 6.2 g

9. Banana Bread

Preparation Time: 10 minutes

Cooking Time: 50 minutes

Servings: 4

Ingredients:

- 3 bananas, peeled
- ⅓ c. melted almond butter
- 1 tsp. baking soda
- Pinch of salt
- ¾ c. Splenda
- 1 egg white, beaten
- 1 tsp. vanilla extract
- 1 ½ c. of coconut flour

Directions:

- Adjust your oven to 350F to preheat.
- Grease a 4x8 inch bread pan with almond butter.
- Mash bananas in a glass bowl and whisk in melted almond butter.
- Mix baking soda with salt in another bowl.
- Add Splenda, vanilla extract, and whisked egg.
- Stir in flour and mix well until smooth.
- Transfer the batter to the greased pan.
- Bake for 50 minutes.
- Slice and serve.

Nutrition: Calories: 387, Total Fat: 6 g, Saturated Fat: 9.9 g , Cholesterol: 41 mg, Sodium: 154 mg, Total Carbs: 37.4 g , Fiber: 2.9 g , Sugar: 15.3 g , Protein: 6.6 g

10. English Muffins

Preparation Time: 10 minutes

Cooking Time: 15 minutes

Servings: 4

Ingredients:

- 1 ¾ c. almond milk
- 3 tbsps. softened almond butter
- 1 ½ tsps. salt, to taste
- 2 tbsps. Splenda
- 1 egg white, lightly beaten
- 4 ½ c. coconut flour
- 2 tsps. instant yeast
- Semolina or farina, for sprinkling the grill or pan

Directions:

- Mix all the muffin ingredients in a mixing bowl except the semolina.
- Blend the ingredients using an electric mixer to form a smooth dough.
- Let the dough rest for 2 hours.
- Grease 2 muffin trays with cooking oil and sprinkle semolina into each cup.
- Knead the raised dough and divide it into 16 equal pieces.
- Roll each piece into small balls.
- Place the balls in the muffin trays and cover them.
- Allow them to rest for 20 minutes.
- Bake for 15 mins on low heat in the preheated oven until golden.
- Serve.

Nutrition:

Calories: 212
Total Fat: 11.8 g
Saturated Fat: 2.2 g
Cholesterol: 0 mg
Sodium: 321 mg
Total Carbs: 14.6 g
Dietary Fiber: 4.4 g
Sugar: 8 g
Protein: 17.3 g

11.Kale Salad

Preparation Time: 30 minutes

Cooking Time: 20 minutes

Servings: 5

Ingredients:

- Salt
- ½ tsp. Orange zest, grated
- 1 tsp. Chopped thyme
- 1 tsp. Dijon mustard
- ¼ c. Plain yogurt
- 1 Chopped carrot
- 3 Chopped radishes
- 2 c. Chopped and steamed kale

Directions:

- Take out a big bowl and toss the carrot, radishes, and kale inside of it.
- Add salt, orange zest, dill, thyme, mustard, and yogurt to a second bowl.
- Toss the dressing in with the salad and then serve right away.

Nutrition:

Calories: 76
Total Fat: 4 g
Saturated Fat: 0.5 g
Fiber: 1.2 g
Sugar: 1 g

12.Steel Cut Oatmeal

Preparation Time: 15 minutes

Cooking Time: 35 minutes

Servings: 1

Ingredients:

- 1 tbsp. almond butter
- 1 c. steel-cut oats
- 3 c. boiling water
- ½ c. almond milk
- ½ c. plus 1 tbsp. cashew milk
- 1 tbsp. Splenda
- ¼ tsp. cinnamon

Directions:

- Heat almond butter with oats in a saucepan.
- Stir cook for 2 minutes, then stirs in boiling water.
- Bring the mixture to a low simmer and cook for 25 minutes.
- Add half of the almond and cashew milk and cook for 10 minutes.
- Stir in all the remaining ingredients.
- Serve.

Nutrition:

Calories: 412

Total Fat: 24.8 g

Saturated Fat: 12.4 g

Cholesterol: 3 mg

Sodium: 132 mg

Total Carbs: 43.8 g

Dietary Fiber: 13.9 g

Sugar: 21.5 g

Protein: 18.9 g

13.Baked Apples With Cinnamon & Ginger

Preparation Time: 10 minutes

Cooking Time: 40 minutes

Servings: 4

Ingredients:

- 4 apples
- 2 ginger, chopped
- ½ tsp. cinnamon
- 4 prunes, chopped
- 50 g muscovado sugar
- 1 tbsp. butter
- Four scoops of vanilla ice cream for serving

Directions:

- Preheat the oven to 200F. Cut the quarter of each apple and set them into a baking dish.
- Take a bowl, add ginger, cinnamon, sugar, prunes, and butter, and mix well. Pour the mixture over the apples and put the butter on each apple's top.
- Bake them for 35 minutes or until cooked well.
- Remove and serve the hot baked cinnamon apple with a scoop of vanilla ice cream.

Nutrition:

Calories: 175

Total Fat: 4 g

Saturated Fat: 0.5 g

Fiber: 1.2 g

Sugar: 1 g

14. Mexican Breakfast Toast

Preparation Time: 5 minutes

Cooking Time: 20 minutes

Servings: 2

Ingredients:

- 2 slices of sprouted bread, toasted
- 2 tbsps. hummus
- ½ c. spinach, chopped
- ¼ red onion, sliced
- ½ c. sprouts
- 1 avocado, thinly sliced
- ¼ tsp. Himalayan salt
- Spicy Yogurt
- 3 tbsps. unsweetened yogurt
- ½ lime, juiced
- 1 tsp. cumin
- 1 tsp. cayenne

Directions:

- In a small bowl, prepare the spicy yogurt by combining all the spicy yogurt ingredients and whisking well to combine.
- Place toast slices on plates and spread a tablespoon of hummus on each. Place spinach on each slice and Spicy Yogurt, red onion, sprouts, and avocado. Sprinkle each with salt and serve.

Nutrition:

Calories: 438kcal

Carbs: 15g

Protein: 23g

Fat: 36g

Saturated Fat: 12g

15.Banana Breakfast Pudding

Preparation Time: 5 minutes plus 8 hours of chill time

Cooking Time: 0 minutes

Servings: 1

Ingredients:

- 1 c. coconut milk
- 1 tbsp. Raw honey
- ½ tsp. Vanilla extract
- ¼ tsp. Cinnamon
- ¼ tsp. Nutmeg
- ⅛ tsp. Himalayan salt
- 2 tbsps. chia seeds
- 1 banana, sliced
- 1 tbsp. walnuts, toasted and crushed
- 1 tbsp. cacao nibs

Directions:

- In a small bowl or jar with a cover, place coconut milk, honey, vanilla, cinnamon, nutmeg, salt, and chia seeds.
- Let sit in the fridge, covered, overnight.
- In the morning, top with banana, walnuts, and cacao nibs before serving.

Nutrition: Calories: 434kcal , Carbs: 27g , Protein: 27g

16. Papaya Breakfast Boat

Preparation Time: 5 minutes

Cooking Time: 0 minutes

Servings: 2

Ingredients:

- 1 papaya, cut lengthwise in half and seeds removed
- 1 c. unsweetened yogurt
- 1 lime, zested
- 3 tbsps. raw oats
- 1 tbsp. unsweetened shredded coconut
- ½ banana, sliced
- ¼ c. raspberries
- 1 tbsp. walnuts, chopped
- 1 tsp. chia seeds
- 1 tsp. raw honey

Directions:

- Place papaya halves on plates and place yogurt on top of each.
- Then top each half with lime zest, oats, coconut, banana, raspberries, walnuts, and chia seeds.
- Drizzle with honey and serve.

Nutrition:

Calories: 60kcal

Carbs: 5g

Protein: 6g

Fat: 3g

Sodium: 90mg

Fiber: 1g

Sugar: 1g

17.Omega-Overnight Oats

Preparation Time: 5 minutes

Cooking Time: 0 minutes

Servings: 2

Ingredients:

- 1 small ripe banana, mashed
- ⅓ c. rolled oats
- ¾ c. unsweetened almond milk
- ½ tsp. Vanilla extract
- ½ tsp. Cinnamon
- ¼ tsp. Nutmeg
- ⅛ tsp. Himalayan salt
- 1 tbsp. chia seeds
- 1 tbsp. ground flaxseeds
- 1 tsp. raw honey
- 1 tbsp. raw almonds, slivered and divided
- ¼ c. blackberries

Directions:

- Place banana, oats, almond milk, vanilla, cinnamon, nutmeg salt, chia seeds, flaxseeds, honey, and half of the almonds in a medium-sized bowl with a lid or a jar. Stir well to combine and cover.
- Leave in the fridge overnight.
- When ready to eat, top with remaining almonds and blackberries.

Nutrition: Calories: 199kcal , Carbs: 1g , Protein: 1g Fat: 22g , Saturated Fat: 3g , Sodium: 23mg , Fiber: 1g , Sugar: 1g

18.Corn Porridge with Maple and Raisins

Preparation Time: 5 minutes

Cooking Time: 0 minutes

Servings: 2

Ingredients:

- ¾ c. cornmeal
- 2¼ c. water, divided
- Pinch salt
- 1 tbsp. pure maple syrup
- 3 tbsps. raisins

Directions:

- Whisk together the cornmeal and ¾ cup of water in a small bowl.
- In a small pot, bring the remaining 1½ cups of water and the salt to a boil over medium-high heat.
- Whisk in the cornmeal slurry. Cook, stirring for 10 to 12 minutes, until thick.
- Stir in the maple syrup and raisins. Then serve hot.

Nutrition:

Calories: 288

Protein: 6 g

Fat: 3 g

Carbs: 60 g

19.Milky Oat

Preparation Time: 8 minutes

Cooking Time: 0 minutes

Servings: 2

Ingredients:

- 1 c. oats
- ½ c. low-fat coconut milk
- ½ c. water
- 1 tsp. liquid stevia

Directions:

- Mix up together the coconut milk and water in the saucepan.
- Add oats and stir.
- Close the lid and cook the oats over medium heat for 10 minutes.
- Let them chill for 5–10 minutes when the oats are cooked.
- Then add liquid stevia and stir it.
- After this, transfer the milky oat to the bowls and serve!

Nutrition:

Calories: 293

Fat: 17 g

Carbs: 31 g

Protein: 6.8 g

20. Mango Salsa

Preparation Time: 15 minutes

Cooking Time: 0 minutes

Servings: 6

Ingredients:

- 1 avocado, peeled, pitted, & cut into cubes
- 2 tbsps. fresh lime juice
- 1 mango, peeled, pitted, and cubed
- 1 c. cherry tomatoes, halved
- 1 jalapeño pepper, seeded and chopped
- 1 tbsp. fresh cilantro, chopped
- Sea salt, to taste

Directions:

- Add the avocado and lime juice to a large bowl and mix well.
- Add the remaining ingredients and stir to combine.
- Serve immediately.

Nutrition:

Calories: 108, Total Fat: 6.8 g, Saturated Fat: 1.4 g, Cholesterol: 0 mg, Sodium: 43 mg , Carbs: 12.6 g, Fiber: 3.6 g , Sugar: 8.7 g, Protein: 1.4 g

CHAPTER 4:
Lunch

21.Beef Massaman Curry

Preparation Time: 10 minutes

Cooking Time: 30 minutes

Servings: 6

Ingredients:

- 1½ tbsps. vegetable oil
- 2 onions, chopped
- 2 ¼ c. Thai jasmine rice
- 2 c. Thai Massaman paste
- 3 c. potatoes, cut into 2cm-thick slices
- 5 ¼ c. cooked roast beef, cut into chunks
- 1 ⅓ c. pack of baby corn and snap peas,

Directions:

- Preheat oil in a deep-frying pan and sauté onions for 10 minutes on low heat.
- Boil rice in salted water for 10 minutes, then drain and keep them aside.
- Add Massaman paste and cook for 1 minute.
- Put in sliced potato, coconut milk, and star anise.
- Cook this mixture for 15 minutes.
- Add snap peas, a splash of water, corn, and beef.
- Cook for 5 mins, then serve.

Nutrition:

Calories: 231

Total Fat: 20.1 g

Saturated Fat: 2.4 g

Cholesterol: 110 mg

Sodium: 941 mg

Carbs: 20.1 g

Fiber: 0.9 g

Sugar: 1.4 g

Protein: 14.6 g

22.Mediterranean Lamb Stew with Olives

Preparation Time: 15 minutes

Cooking Time: 1 hr. 30 minutes

Servings: 4

Ingredients:

- ½ lb. lamb leg steaks, cut into 2½ cm/ 1in chunks
- 1 c. yogurt, plus 4 tbsps. to serve
- 1 tbsp. medium curry powder
- 2 tsp. cold-pressed rapeseed oil
- 2 medium onions, one thinly sliced, 1 cut into five wedges
- 2 garlic cloves, peeled and finely sliced
- 1 tbsp. ginger, peeled and finely chopped
- ¼ c. dried split red lentils, rinsed
- ½ small pack of coriander, roughly chopped, plus extra to garnish
- 1 c. pack baby leaf spinach

Directions:

- Add oil to a suitable pan and heat.
- Sear lamb for 10 minutes until brown. Transfer it to a plate lined with pepper.
- Heat more oil and sauté onion for 5 minutes.
- Stir in garlic and cook for 30 secs.
- Return the lamb to the pan.
- Add thyme, ¾ cup water, and orange peel.
- Let it cook for 1 hour on a low simmer.
- Stir in olives. Cook for 20 minutes, then serve.

Nutrition: Calories: 201

Total Fat: 5.5 g

Saturated Fat: 2.1 g

Cholesterol: 10 mg

Sodium: 597 mg

Carbs: 2.4 g

Fiber: 0 g

Sugar: 0 g

Protein: 3.1g

23.Sweet & Sour Ground Chicken

Preparation Time: 10 minutes

Cooking Time: 13 minutes

Servings: 2

Ingredients:

- 1 tbsp. Extra Virgin Olive Oil
- ½ tsp. Ginger minced
- ¼ c. Fresh Basil, chopped
- ¾ lb. Lean Ground Chicken
- Himalayan Crystal Salt, to taste
- 1 tsp. Honey

Directions:

- In a nonstick skillet, heat the oil on medium heat. Add the ginger and basil, and sauté for about 1 minute.
- Add the chicken and stir fry for about 6 to 7 minutes. Stir in the remaining ingredients and stir for another 4 to 5 minutes. Serve immediately while hot.

Nutrition:

Calories: 176

Total Fat: 9 g

Saturated Fat: 3 g

Cholesterol: 90 mg

24. Turkey with Greens

Preparation Time: 15 minutes

Cooking Time: 18 minutes

Servings: 2

Ingredients:

- 1 tsp. Extra Virgin Olive Oil
- 1 Celery Stalk, minced
- ½ lb. Lean Ground Turkey
- 2 c. Collard Greens
- ½ c. Low-sodium Vegetable Broth
- Himalayan Crystal Salt, to taste
- ¼ tsp. Freshly Ground Cumin

Directions:

- In a pan, heat the oil on medium heat. Add the celery and sauté for 4 minutes.
- Add the turkey and cook, stirring, for 6 to 7 minutes. Add the collard greens, broth, and cumin, and reduce the heat to low. Cook for a further 6 to 7 minutes.
- Season with salt and serve.

Nutrition:

Calories: 290

Total Fat: 9 g

Saturated Fat: 3 g

Cholesterol: 90 mg

25.Grilled Chicken & Spinach

Preparation Time: 10 minutes

Cooking Time: 20 minutes

Servings: 2

Ingredients:

- 1 tbsp. Olive Oil
- 2 (4 oz.) sliced boneless, skinless Chicken Breasts,
- Himalayan Crystal Salt, to taste
- 3 c. Fresh Spinach, trimmed

Directions:

- Preheat the grill to medium heat. Lightly grease the grill grate.
- Coat the chicken with half of the oil and sprinkle with salt. Grill the chicken for approximately 5 minutes on either side. Set aside the chicken onto a plate and cover it with foil to keep it warm.
- Increase the temperature of the grill to medium-high. Place greased foil paper on a smooth surface and place the spinach in the center of the foil. Drizzle with the remaining oil and sprinkle with salt. Fold the foil to seal it. Grill the spinach for about 10 minutes.
- Place the spinach on a serving plate. Place the chicken on top of the spinach and serve.

Nutrition:

Calories: 276

Total Fat: 9 g

Saturated Fat: 3 g

Cholesterol: 90 mg

26. Pepper Steak

Preparation Time: 10 minutes

Cooking Time: 4 hours 10 minutes

Servings: 6

Ingredients:

- 3 tbsps. olive oil
- 2 lbs. beef sirloin, cut into strips
- Garlic powder, to taste
- ¼ c. beef broth
- 1 tbsp. xanthan gum
- ½ c. chopped onion
- 2 large green bell peppers, roughly chopped
- 1 red bell pepper, roughly chopped
- 3 tbsps. soy sauce
- 1 tsp. Splenda
- 1 tsp. salt

Directions:

- Season sirloin with garlic powder and set it aside.
- Heat oil in a pan and sear the beef until brown on both sides.
- Transfer the beef to the slow cooker.
- Dissolve xanthan gum in some water and add it to the cooker.
- Add all the remaining ingredients.
- Cover the dish with the lid, then cook for 4 hours on a high setting.
- Stir well and serve warm.

Nutrition: Calories: 301 , Total Fat: 15.8 g , Saturated Fat: 2.7 g, Cholesterol: 75 mg, Sodium: 1189 mg, Carbs: 11.7 g, Fiber: 0.3g, Sugar: 0.1 g, Protein: 28.2 g

27.Chicken with Kale

Preparation Time: 10 minutes

Cooking Time: 17 minutes

Servings: 2

Ingredients:

- 1 tbsp. Extra Virgin Olive Oil
- 2 (4 oz.) boneless, skinless Chicken Breasts
- Himalayan Crystal Salt, to taste
- 1 c. Fresh Kale, trimmed and torn
- ¼ c. Low-sodium Chicken Broth

Directions:

- In a large skillet, heat the oil on medium heat. Add the chicken and sprinkle with salt. Cook for 4 minutes on either side. Set aside the chicken.
- Add the kale and sauté for about 2 minutes in the same skillet. Add the broth and bring it to a boil on high heat. Reduce the heat to medium-low, cooking for 4 to 5 minutes.
- Return the chicken to the skillet and cook for 2 minutes more. Serve immediately while hot.

Nutrition:

Calories: 189

Total Fat: 9 g

Saturated Fat: 3 g

Cholesterol: 90 mg

28. Cuban Beef and Zucchini Kebabs

Preparation Time: 10 minutes

Cooking Time: 20 minutes

Servings: 4

Ingredients:

- 1 (16 oz.) sirloin steak (1 inch thick), cut into one ¼-inch piece
- 8 (12-inch) wooden skewers
- ½ tsp. Salt
- ¼ tsp. black pepper
- 2 (10 oz.) zucchini, cut on a long diagonal into ½-inch-thick slices
- 2 tbsps. olive oil

Directions:

- Heat the grill on medium-high heat to 375F.
- Thread beef on half of the skewers and season them with salt and pepper.
- Thread zucchini slices on the remaining skewers and brush them with oil.
- Place the skewers on the baking sheet.
- Grill the 4 minutes per side while rotating constantly.
- Grill the zucchini for 5 minutes per side.
- Serve warm.

Nutrition: Calories: 308, Total Fat: 20.5 g , Saturated Fat: 3 g , Cholesterol: 0 mg , Sodium: 688 mg , Carbs: 10.3 g , Sugar: 1.4g , Fiber: 4.3 g , Protein: 49 g

29. Veggie Rice Bowl

Preparation Time: 10 minutes

Cooking Time: 20 minutes

Servings: 4

Ingredients:

- 1 tbsp. vegetable oil
- 1 ½ c. pack Tender stem broccoli tips, halved lengthways
- 1 red bell pepper, seeded and diced
- 1 ¼ c. pack of marinated tofu pieces
- 2 x 2 ¼ c. pouches of microwave rice
- 2 c. frozen peas
- 1 tbsp. sesame seeds
- 3 spring onions, chopped
- 1 garlic clove, crushed
- 2.5cm piece fresh ginger, grated
- 3 tbsps. coconut amino
- 2 tbsps. sweet chili sauce
- 1 tbsp. apple cider vinegar

Directions:

- Preheat oil in a cooking wok.
- Sauté broccoli with pepper for 3 minutes.
- Add diced tofu and cook for 2 minutes.
- Stir in rice and stir cook for 4 minutes. Add peas to cook for another 3 minutes.
- Make the sauce by mixing the sweet chili sauce with the garlic, coconut amino, and vinegar.
- Pour the sauce over the rice mixture and serve with spring onions and sesame seeds.
- Enjoy.

Nutrition:

Calories: 418
Total Fat: 3.8 g
Saturated Fat: 0.7 g
Cholesterol: 2 mg
Sodium: 620 mg
Total Carbs: 13.3 g
Fiber: 2.4 g
Sugar: 1.2 g
Protein: 5.4g

30.Thai Tofu and Red Cabbage Bowl

Preparation Time: 10 minutes

Cooking Time: 40 minutes

Servings: 4

Ingredients:

- 2 c. (10 oz.) easy cook brown rice
- 1 stick of lemongrass halved lengthways

For the Tofu:

- 2 tbsps. groundnut oil
- 3 ¼ c. tofu, cut into 2cm (1in) cubes
- 1 red bird's-eye chili, finely sliced
- 1/6 c. (1 ½ oz.) pieces of ginger, sliced
- 2 cloves garlic, chopped
- 4 spring onions, sliced
- 1 lime, juiced
- 2 tbsps. coconut amino
- ½ small red cabbage, sliced
- ½ c. (3 ½ oz.) snap peas
- 2 tbsps. (½ oz.) basil leaves, sliced
- 4 tbsps. peanuts, toasted and roughly chopped, to serve
- 1 lime, quartered, to serve

Directions:

- Add rice, lemon grass, and 1 pt. Water to a cooking pot.
- Boil the rice, then reduce the heat to cook for 25 minutes until al dente.
- Meanwhile, heat oil in a wok and sauté tofu for 6 minutes.
- Add garlic, spring onion, ginger, and chili. Stir and cook for 1 minute.
- Add coconut amino and lime juice.
- Stir in snap peas and red cabbage. Cook for 3 minutes.
- Add basil, then put off the heat.
- To serve, add rice to the serving bowl and then top them with the tofu mixture.
- Garnish with peanuts.
- Serve.

Nutrition: Calories: 438 , Total Fat: 4.8 g , Saturated Fat: 1.7 g , Cholesterol: 12 mg , Sodium: 520 mg , Total Carbs: 58.3 g , Fiber: 2.3 g , Sugar: 1.2 g , Protein: 2.1

31.Pepper and Onion Tart

Preparation Time: 5 minutes

Cooking Time: 20 minutes

Servings: 4

Ingredients:

- 2 tbsps. vegetable oil
- 2 onions, peeled and finely sliced
- 1 garlic clove, finely sliced
- 3 ⅓ c. (1 sheet) ready-made puff pastry
- 2 c. red bell peppers, sliced
- 2 sprigs thyme
- 1-2 tbsps. apple cider vinegar
- Salt
- Pepper

Directions:

- Set the oven to 400F.
- Preheat a pan with oil and sauté onions until golden and soft.
- Stir in garlic and stir cook for 5 minutes.
- Spread the puff pastry sheet on a lightly floured surface.
- Place the sheet in a greased baking pan and score the edges around the rims.
- Bake the crust for 5 minutes.
- Add onions mixture over the pastry and top it with bell pepper.
- Drizzle thyme leaves, apple cider vinegar, salt, and pepper.
- Bake for 15 minutes at 400F.
- Slice and serve.

Nutrition: Calories: 383 , Total Fat: 5.3 g , Saturated Fat: 3.9 g , Cholesterol: 135 mg , Sodium: 487 mg , Total Carbs: 76.8 g , Fiber: 0.1g , Sugar: 0 g , Protein: 17.7 g

32. Vegan Vegetable Curry

Preparation Time: 10 minutes

Cooking Time: 60 minutes

Servings: 4

Ingredients:

- 1 tbsp. vegetable oil
- 1 large onion, finely chopped
- 5 cm piece ginger, finely chopped
- 2 garlic cloves, finely chopped
- 1 tsp. ground cumin
- 1 tsp. ground coriander
- 1 tsp. ground turmeric
- 1 aubergine, chopped into 1cm pieces
- 1 c. yogurt
- ½ c. vegetable stock
- 1 zucchini chopped into 1 cm pieces
- ½ c. spinach
- 1 ¼ c. peas (fresh or defrosted, if frozen)

Directions:

- Preheat oil in a large cooking pan. Sauté onion for 7 minutes.
- Add ginger and garlic to sauté for 3 minutes.
- Stir in dried spices and chili. Cook for 1 minute.
- Add the aubergine, yogurt, and stock. Cook for 10 minutes.
- Stir in zucchini and continue cooking with the closed lid for 25 minutes.
- Uncover and cook for 10 minutes.
- Add spinach and peas. Cook for 3 minutes.
- Serve.

Nutrition: Calories: 338, Total Fat: 3.8 g , Saturated Fat: 0.7 g , Cholesterol: 22 mg , Sodium: 620 mg , Total Carbs: 58.3 g , Fiber: 2.4 g , Sugar: 1.2 g Protein: 5.4g

33.Herb and Spiced Lamb

Preparation Time: 10 minutes

Cooking Time: 20 minutes

Servings: 4

Ingredients:

- 14 oz. Lamb neck fillet, trimmed of sinew and excess fat
- ½ tbsp. Cumin
- ½ tbsp. ground coriander
- 1 tbsp. toasted coriander seed, bashed
- 2 tbsps. olive oil, plus a drizzle
- 1 bunch of mint leaves picked
- 1 bunch of dill, chopped
- 1 bunch of coriander leaves picked
- 2 c. feta
- 1 pomegranate, seeds only
- Juice of one lemon

Directions:

- Set the oven to 400F.
- Season the lamb with spices.
- Heat oil in a suitable frying pan and sear the lamb for 3 minutes per side.
- Place it on a baking sheet and roast for 10 minutes in the oven.
- Top the lamb with the remaining ingredients and serve.

Nutrition: Calories: 413 , Total Fat: 8.5 g , Saturated Fat: 3.1 g , Cholesterol: 120 mg , Sodium: 497 mg , Carbs: 21.4 g , Fiber: 0.6 g , Sugar: 0.1 g , Protein: 14.1g

34. Easy Turkey Meatloaf "Muffins"

Preparation Time: 5 minutes

Cooking Time: 25 minutes

Servings: 6

Ingredients:

- 18 oz. ground turkey breast
- 3 carrots, peeled and grated
- 1 egg beaten
- 1 tbsp. soy sauce
- 1 tbsp. Dijon mustard
- 1 tsp. fish sauce
- 1 tsp. dried thyme
- 1 tsp. dried rosemary

Directions:

- Preheat the oven to 350°F.
- Mix the turkey, carrots, egg soy sauce, mustard, fish sauce, thyme, and rosemary in a large bowl. Evenly divide the meat-loaf mixture among the cups of a nonstick 6-muffin tin.
- Bake for about 25 minutes until cooked through.
- Tip: Spread one teaspoon of tomato sauce over each meatloaf before baking.

Nutrition:

Calories: 188

Total Fat: 7g

Saturated Fat: 2g

Cholesterol: 90mg

Carbs: 4g

Fiber: 1g

Protein: 26g

Sodium: 342mg

35.Sicilian Seafood Stew

Preparation Time: 10 minutes

Cooking Time: 25 minutes

Servings: 4

Ingredients:

- 2 tbsps. olive oil
- 1 onion, chopped
- 2 sticks of celery, chopped
- 2 garlic cloves, chopped, plus an extra clove
- 1 anchovy, rinsed
- 1 tsp. dried chili flakes
- 1 c. red bell pepper
- ½ c. nonfat yogurt
- 2 c. vegetable stock
- 3 c. raw peeled prawns
- 2 c. of new potatoes
- Zest and juice of 1 lemon
- 1 tsp. baby capers
- 1 tsp. Flat leaf parsley, chopped

Directions:

- Preheat olive oil in a suitable pot and sauté celery, onion, anchovy, garlic, and chili.
- Season with pepper and salt. Stir and cook for 5 mins.
- Meanwhile, boil potatoes until al dente. Cut them into thick slices.
- Add stock, yogurt, and bell pepper to the pan and cook for 15 minutes.
- Place prawns in the pan, potatoes, capers, lemon zest, and juice.
- Cook for 5 mins, then serve.

Nutrition: Calories: 557 , Total Fat: 29 g , Saturated Fat: 22 g , Cholesterol: 55o mg , Sodium: 1800 mg , Total Carbs: 25 g , Fiber: 3 g , Sugar: 0.3 g , Protein: 47 g

36.White Bean, Chicken, and Rosemary Casserole

Preparation Time: 10 minutes

Cooking Time: 20 minutes

Servings: 4

Ingredients:

- 8 oz. cooked boneless skinless chicken breast
- 2 c. canned white beans, drained
- 2 c. Mushroom Gravy (here)
- 2 tsps. Dried rosemary
- ½ tsp. sea salt

Directions:

- Preheat the oven to 350°F.
- Mix the chicken, beans, gravy, rosemary, and salt in a large bowl. Spoon the mixture evenly into four (6 to 8 oz.) ramekins.
- Bake for 20 minutes.

Tip: Sprinkle one tablespoon of grated Parmesan cheese (if you tolerate it well) on top of each ramekin before baking.

Nutrition:

Calories: 565

Total Fat: 16g

Saturated Fat: 5g

Cholesterol: 160mg

Carbs: 37g

Fiber: 8g

Protein: 66g

Sodium: 671mg

37.Seafood Paella Recipe

Preparation Time: 10 minutes

Cooking Time: 40 minutes

Servings: 4

Ingredients:

- 1 ½ pt. fish stock
- A pinch of saffron
- 1 ½ tbsps. extra-virgin olive oil
- 1 large onion, finely chopped
- 3 crushed garlic cloves
- 1 ¼oz pack of flatleaf parsley, leaves chopped
- 1 tsp. black pepper
- 2 ¼ c. (8 oz.) Spanish paella rice
- 1 c. red bell pepper, chopped
- 1 x 2¼ c. jar roasted peppers, drain and rinse them
- 1 ⅓ c. (6 oz.) raw black tiger prawns
- 1 ¼ c. (5 oz.) live mussels, cleaned and debearded
- 1 ¼ c. raw squid rings
- 1 lemon, cut into wedges

Directions:

- Boil fish stock with saffron and keep it aside.
- Preheat the oil to sauté the onion for 5 minutes.
- Add garlic, bell pepper, parsley, and black pepper. Stir and cook for 2 minutes.
- Stir in rice and stock and cook for 10 minutes.
- Add in roasted peppers and cook for 5 minutes.
- Place prawns, mussels, and squid rings in the pan.
- Cook for 5 mins, then place off the heat.
- Cover the pan with foil and let it sit for 5 minutes.
- Garnish with parsley.
- Serve.

Nutrition: Calories: 272 , Total Fat: 11 g , Saturated Fat: 3 g , Cholesterol: 66 mg , Sodium: 288 mg , Total Carbs: 10 g , Fiber: 4g , Sugar: 0 g , Protein: 33 g

38.Chicken and Fennel Sauté

Preparation Time: 5 minutes

Cooking Time: 8 minutes

Servings: 4

Ingredients:

- 2 tbsps. extra-virgin olive oil
- 1 fennel bulb, thinly sliced
- 12 oz. boneless skinless chicken breast, chopped into ½-inch pieces
- ½ tsp. sea salt
- ½ c. Poultry Broth (here)
- 1 tsp. Dijon mustard
- 1 tsp. dried thyme
- 1 tsp. Grated orange zest

Directions:

- Heat the oil in a 12-inch nonstick sauté pan or skillet over medium-high heat until it shimmers.
- Add the fennel, chicken, and salt. Cook for about 5 minutes, occasionally stirring, until the chicken is cooked.
- Whisk together the broth, mustard, thyme, and orange zest in a small bowl. Stir this into the chicken and fennel. Cook for about 2 minutes, occasionally stirring, until warmed through.

Tip: Fennel resembles celery but with lacy leaves. Remove the celery-like stalks and set them aside for another use. For the bulb, halve it lengthwise and use a paring knife to cut the core out of the bottom of the bulb on each side. From there, thinly slice.

Nutrition: Calories: 247 , Total Fat: 14g , Saturated Fat: 2g , Cholesterol: 76mg , Carbs: 5g , Fiber: 2g , Protein: 26g , Sodium: 513mg

39.Avocado Cream & Noodles

Preparation Time: 20 minutes

Cooking Time: 10 minutes

Servings: 8

Ingredients: (1 portion)

- 1 zucchini
- ½ avocado (100g)
- 20 basil leaves
- 1 ½ tbsps. olive oil
- 3 brown mushrooms (30g)
- 1 garlic clove
- 1 tsp. lemon juice
- ¼ tsp. salt

Directions:

- Spiralize your zucchini. Slice the mushrooms in half.
- Add the avocado, basil, 1 tablespoon olive oil, garlic, lemon juice, and salt to a stick blender cup. Press the button on the stick blender for about a minute until everything is super creamy and delicious.
- Add ½ tablespoon olive oil to a frying pan and cook the mushrooms until tender. Add the zucchini noodles and cook for a minute or so until they get hot.
- Add the avocado cream, mix everything and serve.

Nutrition:

Calories: 350

Fat: 25 g

Carbs: 28.1 g

Sugar: 3.5 g

Protein: 7.1 g

Cholesterol: 23 mg

40.Spaghetti with Watercress and Pea Pesto

Preparation Time: 10 minutes

Cooking Time: 30 minutes

Servings: 4

Ingredients:

- 2 c. frozen peas
- 2 garlic cloves
- ¼ c. watercress
- 2 tbsps. hazelnuts, toasted
- ¼ c. vegetarian hard cheese
- 2 tbsps. olive oil
- 3 ¼ c. whole meal spaghetti
- 4 egg whites

Directions:

- Heat water to a simmer in a cooking pan, and then add garlic and peas.
- Cook for 3 minutes, drain, and then set it aside.
- Blend peas with garlic, watercress, cheese, and hazelnuts until they form a thick paste.
- Add olive oil and blend again until smooth.
- Meanwhile, boil spaghetti as per the instructions, then drain and keep it aside.
- Add water to a suitable cooking pot and bring it to a simmer.
- Create a whirlpool in the water and put egg whites into it. Cook for 3 minutes.
- Mix pesto with spaghetti and serve with poached egg whites, black pepper, and watercress on top.

Nutrition: Calories: 341 , Total Fat: 4 g , Saturated Fat: 0.5 g , Cholesterol: 69 mg , Sodium: 547 mg , Total Carbs: 16.4 g , Fiber: 1.2 g , Sugar: 1 g , Protein: 0.3 g

CHAPTER 5:
Dinner

41. Brown Rice Chicken Salad

Preparation Time: 15 minutes

Cooking Time: 25 minutes

Servings: 5

Ingredients:

- 2 tbsps. chopped fresh basil leaves
- 2 c. cooked chicken, cooled and coarsely chopped
- 1 ½ c. cooked brown rice, cooled
- 1 c. fresh mango, peeled and chopped
- 4 large green lettuce leaves, washed and dried
- ⅓ c. crumbled goat cheese

Directions:

- At the bottom of a large bowl, add basil, chicken, brown rice, and mango. Toss well to combine.
- Garnish with crumbled goat cheese and serve on top of a lettuce leaf.

Nutrition:

Calories: 485

Total Fat: 9 g

Saturated Fat: 3 g

Cholesterol: 90 mg

42. Mushroom Risotto

Preparation Time: 10 minutes

Cooking Time: 20 minutes

Servings: 2

Ingredients:

- 2 tbsps. dried porcini mushrooms
- 1½ tbsps. olive oil
- 1 ¼ c. pack chestnut mushrooms, sliced
- 1 small onion, finely diced
- 1 garlic clove, crushed
- 1 1/6 c. Arborio rice
- ⅓ c. broth
- ½ c. baby spinach
- ¼ c. feta, crumbled

Directions:

- Add dried mushrooms to the boiled water and keep it aside.
- Heat 1 tablespoon oil in a deep pan and sauté chestnut mushrooms for 5 minutes.
- Keep the sautéed mushrooms aside.
- Add ½ tablespoon more oil to the pan. Sauté garlic and onions for 6 minutes.
- Strain dried mushrooms and chop them roughly.
- Add mushrooms to the pan along with rice and broth.
- Cook until the liquid is absorbed, and then return the chestnut mushrooms to the mixture.
- Add reserved mushroom liquid and continue cooking until all the liquid is absorbed.
- Stir in spinach and cook for 2 minutes.
- Serve.

Nutrition:

Calories: 372

Total Fat: 11.8 g

Saturated Fat: 4.4 g

Cholesterol: 62 mg

Sodium: 871 mg

Total Carbs: 11.8 g

Fiber: 0.6 g

Sugar: 7.3 g

Protein: 4 g

43.Barbecued Rump of Beef in Dijon

Preparation Time: 10 minutes

Cooking Time: 15 minutes

Servings: 4

Ingredients:

- 2 lbs. beef top rump joint
- 2 tbsps. fresh tarragon, roughly chopped
- 2 tsp. black pepper
- 1 tbsp. Dijon mustard
- 2 tbsps. olive oil

Directions:

- Keep the meat in a shallow dish and toss with tarragon, mustard, oil, and pepper to season.
- Marinate the meat for 1.5 hours in the refrigerator.
- Preheat the grill and grill for 15 minutes.
- Carve and serve.

Nutrition:

Calories: 280
Total Fat: 3.5 g
Saturated Fat: 0.1 g
Cholesterol: 320 mg
Sodium: 350 mg
Carbs: 7.6 g
Fiber: 0.7 g
Sugar: 0.7 g
Protein: 11.2 g

44. Pan Seared Tuna

Preparation Time: 10 minutes

Cooking Time: 5 minutes

Servings: 2

Ingredients:

- 2 (5 oz.) yellow tuna steaks
- 1 tbsp. extra virgin olive oil
- Himalayan crystal salt, to taste

Directions:

- Evenly coat the fish steaks with oil. Sprinkle the fish with salt.
- Lightly grease a nonstick frying pan with cooking spray and heat it. Place the fish steaks in the pan and cook for 5 minutes, turning after 2½ minutes.

Nutrition:

Calories: 276

Total Fat: 9 g

Saturated Fat: 3 g

Cholesterol: 90 mg

45.Sautéed Chicken with Zucchini

Preparation Time: 10 minutes

Cooking Time: 10 minutes

Servings: 2

Ingredients:

- ½ tbsp. extra virgin olive oil
- ½ lb. lean ground chicken
- 2 small zucchinis, cubed
- Himalayan crystal salt, to taste

Directions:

- In a skillet, heat the oil on medium heat. Add the chicken and sauté for 4 to 5 minutes.
- Add the zucchini and sauté for a further 4 to 5 minutes.
- Season with salt and serve.

Nutrition:

Calories: 325

Total Fat: 9 g

Saturated Fat: 3 g

Cholesterol: 90 mg

46. Beef Curry

Preparation Time: 10 minutes

Cooking Time: 25 minutes

Servings: 4

Ingredients:

- 14 oz. beef rump, sliced thinly
- ¼ c. sunflower oil
- 1 c. brown rice
- 4 ¼ c. boiling water
- 1 tbsp. fresh ginger, minced
- A few slices of fresh ginger
- 2 cloves garlic, minced
- 1 tsp. ground cumin
- 1 tsp. ground coriander
- 1 tsp. turmeric
- 1 tsp. Ground black pepper
- ½ tsp. Chili powder
- ½ tsp. ground ginger
- ½ c. frozen peas
- A few sprigs of coriander to garnish
- Salt

Directions:

- Boil rice in salted water and cook for 12 minutes. Drain and keep aside.
- Preheat sunflower oil in the pan and sear the beef until brown.
- Remove the beef to the plate lined with a paper towel.
- Add ginger and garlic, and sauté for a few minutes.
- Stir in spices and water.
- Cook for 10 minutes, then add peas.
- Adjust seasoning and garnish with coriander.
- Serve.

Nutrition:

Calories: 301

Total Fat: 15.8 g

Saturated Fat: 2.7 g

Cholesterol: 75 mg

Sodium: 1189 mg

Carbs: 11.7 g

Fiber: 0.3g

Sugar: 0.1 g

Protein: 28.2 g

47.Grilled Chicken with Thyme

Preparation Time: 10 minutes

Cooking Time: 16 minutes

Servings: 2

Ingredients:

- 2 (4 oz.) boneless, skinless chicken breasts
- Himalayan crystal salt, to taste
- 2 sprigs of fresh thyme

Directions:

- Preheat the grill to medium-high heat. Grease the grill grate.
- Sprinkle the chicken breasts with salt. Place one thyme sprig over each chicken breast and tie it with a kitchen string.
- Grill for 8 minutes on either side.

Nutrition:

Calories: 302

Total Fat: 9 g

Saturated Fat: 3 g

Cholesterol: 90 mg

48. Flank Steak

Preparation Time: 10 minutes

Cooking Time: 20 minutes

Servings: 4

Ingredients:

- ¼ c. honey
- ¼ c. soy sauce
- ½ c. red wine
- 1 clove of garlic, crushed
- A pinch of dried rosemary, crushed
- A pinch of hot chili powder (optional)
- A pinch of freshly ground black pepper
- 1 lb. flank steak

Directions:

- Mix a bowl of red wine, honey, soy sauce, rosemary, chili powder, pepper, and garlic.
- Pour this marinade over the steak and let it marinate for 24 hours.
- Preheat the grill over high heat and grease its grilling grate with oil.
- Grill the steak for 7 mins per side.
- Serve.

Nutrition:

Calories: 231

Total Fat: 20.1 g

Saturated Fat: 2.4 g

Cholesterol: 110 mg

Sodium: 941 mg

Carbs: 20.1 g

Fiber: 0.9 g

Sugar: 1.4 g

Protein: 14.6 g

49. Marinated Lamb Steaks

Preparation Time: 10 minutes

Cooking Time: 30 minutes

Servings: 6

Ingredients:

- 6 lamb leg steaks
- ½ c. dark coconut aminos
- 1 tbsp. curry powder
- 1 tsp. ground ginger
- 1 tbsp. nonfat yogurt
- 1 tbsp. olive oil
- Salt
- Pepper
- 2 c. of new potatoes
- ⅔ c. pot natural yogurt
- 1 bunch mint
- 1 bunch of spring onions

Directions:

- Combine everything for the marinade and rub it over the lamb steaks.
- Let it marinate for 1 hour at room temperature.
- Meanwhile, boil the potatoes in the salted water, drain them, and let them cool down.
- Mix yogurt with spring onion and mint.
- Toss in potatoes and seasonings.
- Preheat the grill and grill the lamb steaks for 3 minutes per side.
- Serve with potatoes mixture.

Nutrition: Calories: 413, Total Fat: 7.5 g , Saturated Fat: 1.1 g , Cholesterol: 20 mg , Sodium: 97 mg , Carbs: 41.4 g , Fiber: 0 g , Sugar: 0 g , Protein: 21.1g

50. Roast Rib of Beef

Preparation Time: 10 minutes

Cooking Time: 45 minutes

Servings: 6

Ingredients:

- 2 Knorr beef stock cubes
- 1 tbsp. olive oil
- 3 lbs. rib of beef
- 5 small leeks
- 6 parsnips, peeled and halved
- 6 carrots, peeled and halved
- 4 shallots, peeled and halved
- Celery sticks cut into large chunks
- Fresh sage leaves

Directions:

- Set the oven to 400F.
- Mix 1 Knorr beef cube with one tablespoon of oil and rub this paste onto the beef.
- Sear the beef in a greased pan until brown, then transfer them to a roasting pan.
- Sauté leeks in the same pan until golden and place them around the beef.
- Now sauté carrots and parsnips in the pan and transfer them to the roasting pan.
- Top the beef with sage, celery, and shallots.
- Bake for 45 minutes.
- Serve.

Nutrition:

Calories: 472

Total Fat: 11.1 g

Saturated Fat: 5.8 g

Cholesterol: 610 mg

Sodium: 749 mg

Carbs: 19.9 g

Fiber: 0.2 g

Sugar: 0.2 g

Protein: 13.5 g

51.Rosemary Broiled Shrimp

Preparation Time: 10 minutes

Cooking Time: 4 minutes

Servings: 2

Ingredients:

- ¾ lb. large shrimps, shelled and deveined
- 1 tsp. Extra virgin olive oil
- Himalayan crystal salt, to taste
- ½ tsp. dried rosemary, crushed

Directions:

- Preheat the broiler and place the rack 4-inches from the heat. Line a baking tray with foil.
- Place the shrimp on the prepared baking tray in a single layer. Drizzle with the oil. With the rosemary and salt, sprinkle over the shrimp.
- Broil for about 3 to 4 minutes. Remove from the heat and serve.

Nutrition:

Calories: 244

Total Fat: 9 g

Saturated Fat: 3 g

Cholesterol: 90 mg

52. Turkey Stew

Preparation Time: 15 minutes

Cooking Time: 22 minutes

Servings: 2

Ingredients:

- 1 tsp. extra virgin olive oil
- 1 celery stalk, minced
- ¼ tsp. Freshly ground coriander
- ½ tsp. freshly ground cumin
- ½ lb. lean ground turkey
- ½ c. Low-sodium Vegetable Broth
- Himalayan crystal salt, to taste

Directions:

- In a pan, heat the oil on medium heat. Add the celery and sauté for 4 minutes. Add the coriander and cumin, and sauté for a further minute.
- Add the turkey and cook, stirring, for 6 to 7 minutes. Add the remaining ingredients. Increase the heat and bring the pan to a boil. Once boiling, cover and simmer for about 8-10 minutes.

Nutrition:

Calories: 286

Total Fat: 9 g

Saturated Fat: 3 g

Cholesterol: 90 mg

53.Oat and Chickpea Dumplings

Preparation Time: 5 minutes

Cooking Time: 15 minutes

Servings: 4

Ingredients:

- 6 tbsps. rapeseed oil
- 2 medium onions, finely chopped
- 2 tsp. ground cumin
- 2 cans of chickpeas, drained
- 1 pack coriander
- ½ c. oats
- 2 c. passata with onion and garlic

Directions:

- Grease a frying pan with two tablespoons of oil and sauté onions for 5 minutes until golden.
- Stir in cumin and cook for 1 minute, then keep the mixture in a food processor.
- Add coriander, chickpeas, seasoning, and two tablespoons of oil. Blend until smooth.
- Fold in oats and make 16 small balls from it.
- Heat oil for frying and cook the dumpling for 3 minutes.
- Stir in passata along with water and let it simmer for 2 minutes.
- Serve warm.

Nutrition:

Calories: 198

Total Fat: 3.8 g

Saturated Fat: 5.1 g

Cholesterol: 20 mg

Sodium: 272 mg

Total Carbs: 3.6 g

Fiber: 1 g

Sugar: 1.3 g

Protein: 1.8 g

54.Lamb Kofta Curry

Preparation Time: 10 minutes

Cooking Time: 50 minutes

Servings: 4

Ingredients:

- 2 tbsps. olive oil
- 2 red onions, finely chopped
- 3-4 long green chili peppers, deseeded, finely chopped
- 4 garlic cloves, chopped
- 5cm piece root ginger, grated
- 2 tsp. ground cumin
- 1 tsp. turmeric
- 1 tsp. ground coriander
- 2 c. minced lamb
- ½ c. fine fresh white breadcrumbs
- 2 tbsps. chopped coriander
- 1 egg beaten
- 2 tsp. Panch Phoron seasoning
- 2 c. non-fat yogurt
- 1 c. hot vegetable stock
- 2 bay leaves
- 4 tbsps. coconut cream

Directions:

- Preheat the grill to medium heat.
- Heat oil in a suitable frying pan and sauté ginger, garlic, onions, and chili for 5 minutes.
- Reserve half this mixture and add turmeric, coriander ground, and cumin.

74

- Cook for 1 minute, then remove it from the heat.
- Mix minced meat with coriander, egg, and breadcrumbs.
- Toss in onion mix and make small balls from this mixture.
- Arrange the lamb meatballs in the baking dish and grill for 15 minutes.
- Make the sauce by mixing onion mixture and Panch phiran. Cook for 2 minutes.
- Add yogurt, stock, seasoning, and bay leaves. Cook for 15 minutes.
- Discard the bay leaves and stir in coconut cream.
- Blend the mixture, then add meatballs. Cook for 10 minutes.
- Serve.

Nutrition:

Calories: 253

Total Fat: 7.5 g

Saturated Fat: 1.1 g

Cholesterol: 20 mg

Sodium: 297 mg

Carbs: 10.4 g

Fiber: 0 g

Sugar: 0 g

Protein: 13.1g

55. Vegetarian Pasta Bakes with Halloumi

Preparation Time: 10 minutes

Cooking Time: 40 minutes

Servings: 4

Ingredients:

- 2 c. conchiglie pasta
- 2 c. frozen broad beans
- ⅔ c. mascarpone
- ¼ c. pack watercress
- 1 lemon, zested
- 2 x 1 1/6 c. packs chargrilled artichokes, thinly sliced
- 1 ⅓ c. halloumi, cubed
- 1 large red chili, sliced (optional)

Directions:

- Set the oven to 400F. Meanwhile, boil salted water in a pan.
- Add pasta to the water and cook for 10 minutes. Stir in broad beans.
- Cook for 2 minutes, then adds mascarpone.
- Chop watercress and add it to the pasta, along with lemon zest and seasoning.
- Spread half of the pasta mixture in a baking dish and top it with sliced artichokes.
- Add the remaining half of the pasta. Top it with halloumi cubes.
- Bake for 30 minutes.
- Garnish as desired and serve.

Nutrition:

Calories: 311

Total Fat: 0.5 g

Saturated Fat: 2.4 g

Cholesterol: 69 mg

Sodium: 58 mg

Total Carbs: 1.4 g

Fiber: 0.7 g

Sugar: 0.3 g

Protein: 1.4 g

56.Broccoli Pesto Penne with Chili and Garlic

Preparation Time: 10 minutes

Cooking Time: 15 minutes

Servings: 2

Ingredients:

- 1 ¼ c. whole wheat penne
- 2 c. broccoli florets
- 2 tbsps. basil
- 2 tbsps. flat-leaf parsley
- 2 tsps. roasted chopped hazelnuts
- 3 tsp. olive oil
- 2 tbsps. vegetarian hard cheese
- 2 garlic cloves, thinly sliced
- 1 large red chili, sliced into thin rounds

Directions:

- Boil penne pasta as per the given instruction on the pack.
- Blanch broccoli for 3 minutes in hot water and then drain.
- Grind broccoli with parsley, basil, oil, and nuts in a processor.
- Add cheese and the cooking water, and seasoning tablespoons to the blender.
- Drain the pasta and add it to a bowl while tossing it with broccoli pesto.
- Heat oil in a cooking pan and sauté garlic with chili for 1 minute.
- Serve pasta with sautéed garlic mixture.
- Garnish as desired.
- Enjoy.

Nutrition: Calories: 304 , Total Fat: 30.6 g , Saturated Fat: 13.1 g , Cholesterol: 131 mg , Sodium: 834 mg , Total Carbs: 21.4g , Fiber: 0.2 g , Sugar: 0.3 g , Protein: 4.6 g

57. Vegan Shepherd's Pie

Preparation Time: 10 minutes

Cooking Time: 45 minutes

Servings: 4

Ingredients:

- 3 ⅔ c. miniature potatoes
- 2 tbsps. flat-leaf parsley, finely chopped
- 3 tbsps. olive oil
- 1 onion, finely chopped
- 2 c. closed c. mushrooms, halved and thinly sliced
- 2 garlic cloves, finely chopped
- ¼ tsp. crushed chilies
- 2 ¼ c. ready-to-eat puy lentils
- 2 c. chopped red bell pepper
- 2 tbsps. yogurt

Directions:

- Boil potatoes for 15 minutes until al dente; drain and return to the pot.
- Crush the potatoes lightly while seasoning them with spices and parsley.
- Preheat 2 tablespoons of oil in a deep pan. Sauté onion for 3 minutes.
- Increase the heat to sauté mushrooms for 7 minutes.
- Add chilies, garlic, puree, lentil, and water to the pot. Cook for 10 minutes.
- Season the mixture and add parsley.
- Preheat the grill to high heat.
- Spread the mushroom mixture in a baking dish. Top it with crushed potatoes evenly.
- Drizzle the remaining oil and grill for 10 minutes.
- Serve.

Nutrition:

Calories: 246
Total Fat: 14.8 g
Saturated Fat: 0.7 g
Cholesterol: 22 mg
Sodium: 220 mg
Total Carbs: 40.3 g
Fiber: 2.4 g
Sugar: 1.2 g
Protein: 12.4g

58.Seafood Stew

Preparation Time: 05 minutes

Cooking Time: 20 minutes

Servings: 4

Ingredients:

- 1 large onion, finely sliced
- 1 garlic clove, finely chopped
- Black pepper, to taste
- 1 c. nonfat yogurt
- 2 c. chicken stock
- 4 ¼ c. skinless white fish fillets, chopped into large chunks
- 1 ⅓ c. raw peeled king prawns
- 2 c. mussels, cleaned and debearded
- Small bunch of flat-leaf parsley leaves roughly chopped
- Crusty bread and almond butter, to serve (optional)

Directions:

- Preheat oil in a pan and sauté for onions for 5 minutes.
- Add pepper and garlic, stir cook for 2 minutes.
- Pour in stock and yogurt. Cook for 10 minutes.
- Place fish chunks in the pan and cook for 2 minutes.
- Stir in mussels and prawns. Cover the pan and cook for 3 minutes.
- Garnish with parsley.
- Serve.

Nutrition: Calories: 301 , Total Fat: 12.2 g , Saturated Fat: 2.4 g , Cholesterol: 110 mg , Sodium: 276 mg , Total Carbs: 5 g , Fiber: 0.9 g , Sugar: 1.4 g , Protein: 28.8 g

59. Fritto Misto with Gremolata

Preparation Time: 5 minutes

Cooking Time: 15 minutes

Servings: 4

Ingredients:

- Small bunch of flat-leaf parsley, finely chopped
- 1 lemon zest
- ½ tsp. Garlic, finely chopped

For the Frito Misto:

- ⅓ c. (3 oz.) almond flour
- ¼ tsp. black pepper
- 2 ¼ c. cod fillet, bones removed and cut into bite-sized pieces
- 1 ⅓ c. mixed seafood
- 6 tbsps. olive oil
- Good quality mayo to serve

Directions:

- Mix all the ingredients for gremolata.
- Combine flour with black pepper and seasoning in a bowl.
- Dip the seafood into the flour mixture.
- Preheat oil in a frying pan and fry the coated seafood until golden brown.
- Serve.

Nutrition:

Calories: 310

Total Fat: 2.4 g

Saturated Fat: 0.1 g

Cholesterol: 320 mg

Sodium: 350 mg

Total Carbs: 12.2 g

Fiber: 0.7 g

Sugar: 0.7 g

Protein: 44.3 g

60.Fritto Misto

Preparation Time: 5 minutes

Cooking Time: 10 minutes

Servings: 2

Ingredients:

- Vegetable oil for deep frying
- 1 egg
- ½ pt. whole milk
- 1 lb. mixed raw seafood, cut into pieces
- 1 zucchini, cut into batons
- ⅔ c. (4 oz.) almond flour
- 6 tbsps. corn flour
- ⅔ c. (4 oz.) semolina

Directions:

- Preheat the oil to 320F in a deep pan.
- Beat milk with egg white and seasonings.
- Add seafood and zucchini to the milk.
- Combine corn flour, semolina, and flour in a bowl.
- Dip the seafood and zucchini in the flour mixture and shake off the excess.
- Add oil to a deep and heat to frying until golden.
- Serve.

Nutrition: Calories: 372 , Total Fat: 1.1 g , Saturated Fat: 3.8 g , Cholesterol: 10 mg , Sodium: 749 mg , Total Carbs: 4.9 g , Fiber: 0.2 g , Sugar: 0.2 g , Protein: 33.5 g

CHAPTER 6:
Dessert

61.Spiced Walnuts

Preparation Time: 5 minutes

Cooking Time: 15 minutes

Servings: 4

Ingredients:

- 24 Shelled walnuts
- ¼ tsp. Ground cloves
- ½ tsp. Ground ginger
- ¼ c. Dark brown sugar
- 2 tbsps. Butter

Directions:

- Take a skillet to start this one, and melt the butter inside with the skillet on the stove.
- You can add the cloves, ginger, and brown sugar when the butter is melted. Cook this, making sure to stir along the way as it boils.
- When this time is done, you can add the walnuts and let them cook for a bit.
- After three more minutes of cooking, take the walnuts off the heat and allow them some time to cool down before serving.

Nutrition:

Calories: 143

Total Fat: 4 g

Saturated Fat: 0.5 g

Fiber: 1.2 g

Sugar: 1 g

62.Cinnamon Popcorn

Preparation Time: 10 minutes

Cooking Time: 20 minutes

Servings: 4

Ingredients:

- 2 tbsps. Butter, melted
- 6 c. Popcorn, air-popped
- ¼ c. Sugar

Directions:

- Take out a small bowl and combine the cinnamon and sugar well.
- When that is done, pop the popcorn until it is all done. Then add it to a really big bowl.
- Toss in the sugar and cinnamon mixture along with the melted butter. Stir it all around to coat all of your popcorn with the cinnamon and the sugar, and then serve right away.

Nutrition:

Calories: 187

Total Fat: 4 g

Saturated Fat: 0.5 g

Fiber: 1.2 g

Sugar: 1 g

63.Baked Chips

Preparation Time: 10 minutes

Cooking Time: 20 minutes

Servings: 6

Ingredients:

- ½ tsp. Salt
- 1 Tbsp. Olive oil
- 1 Sliced Yukon Gold potatoes

Directions:

- To start this recipe, turn on the oven and give it time to heat up to 400 F.
- While the oven takes some time to heat up, bring out a bit bowl and toss the slices of potatoes inside.
- Mix in the salt and the oil, tossing everything around to ensure the potato slices are covered.
- When that is done, take a baking sheet with a rim and spread your potato slices in a single layer. Add to the oven to bake for a bit.
- After about 15 minutes, the potato slices should be nice and crisp. Take them out and let them cool down before serving.

Nutrition:

Calories: 128

Total Fat: 4 g

Saturated Fat: 0.5 g

Fiber: 1.2 g

Sugar: 1 g

64.Carob and Peanut Butter Balls

Preparation Time: 15 minutes

Cooking Time: 0 minutes

Servings: 4

Ingredients:

- Salt
- 1 Tbsp. Carob powder, unsweetened
- 3 tbsps. Confectioners' sugar
- 6 tbsps. Crunchy peanut butter

Directions:

- Take a medium bowl and combine the salt carob powder, confectioner's sugar, and peanut butter.
- When those ingredients are combined, you can roll the mixture into six balls.
- Put into the fridge to chill for a bit before serving.

Nutrition:

Calories: 140

Total Fat: 1.8 g

Saturated Fat: 0.7 g

Cholesterol: 2 mg

65. Yogurt and Melon Ice Pops

Preparation Time: 15 minutes

Cooking Time: 0 minutes

Servings: 4

Ingredients:

- 2 tbsps. Maple syrup, pure
- 1 c. Plain yogurt
- 2 c. Honeydew balls

Directions:

- Bring out a blender or a food processor and combine all your ingredients. You will need to process these together until they can become smooth.
- When this is done, bring out an ice pop mold with at least four parts. Pour your mixture inside as evenly as possible.
- Add these to the freezer and let them sit for 8 hours or more until they are nice and frozen. Serve when ready.

Nutrition:

Calories: 59

Total Fat: 1.8 g

Saturated Fat: 0.7 g

Cholesterol: 2 mg

66. Banana Dessert

Preparation Time: 10 minutes

Cooking Time: 10 minutes

Servings: 2

Ingredients:

- 3 tbsps. Sugar
- 1 Banana

Directions:

- Turn on the broiler and give it some time to heat up to a high setting.
- While the oven takes some time to heat up, take the banana and peel it. Then slice it in half, going horizontally.
- Cut each of the halves into half, going lengthwise as well. Then add these pieces onto a rimmed baking sheet, making sure the cut side is up.
- When this is done, add some sugar over the bananas before putting the baking sheet into the oven.
- You will want to check on the bananas regularly to ensure they will not burn.
- After about four to five minutes, the sugar should start to melt and brown. This is how we know the bananas are done.
- Take them out of the oven and serve once they have some time to cool down.

Nutrition:

Calories: 55

Total Fat: 1.8 g

Saturated Fat: 0.7 g

Cholesterol: 2 mg

67. Almond Meringue Cookies

Preparation Time: 10 minutes

Cooking Time: 30 minutes

Servings: 6

Ingredients:

- ¾ c. Sugar
- Salt
- ¼ tsp. Cream of tartar
- ¼ tsp. Orange zest, grated
- 1 tsp. Almond extract
- 2 Egg whites

Directions:

- Turn on the oven to start this recipe and give it some time to heat to 300F. While the oven is warming, use some parchment paper to line the baking sheet and set this to the side.
- When you are ready, bring out a large bowl and add in the salt, cream of tartar, orange zest, almond extract, and egg whites.
- Take out your electric mixture and start beating these ingredients together, going on a high setting until the mixture starts to make some stiff peaks.
- With the mixer still running, add in the sugar, going in a thin little stream until it has time to get into the bowl.
- When this is done, spoon the meringue into 12 mounds on that baking sheet with parchment paper.
- Add the cookies into the oven and let them bake. You want to ensure that the cookies are brown and become crispy.
- After 25 minutes, the cookies should be done. Take them out of the oven and give them time to cool down before serving.

Nutrition:

Calories: 80

Total Fat: 1.8 g

Saturated Fat: 0.7 g

Cholesterol: 2 mg

68.Peanut Butter Cookies

Preparation Time: 10 minutes

Cooking Time: 30 minutes

Servings: 4

Ingredients:

- 1 Egg
- 1 c. Brown sugar
- 1 c. Peanut butter

Directions:

- To start this recipe, turn on the oven and let it heat up to 350F. While the oven is warming up, take out a baking sheet that you want to use and top it with some parchment paper.
- You can then take out a medium bowl and add the egg, brown sugar, and peanut butter of your choice. Cream these together until you get all the ingredients to mix well.
- After this, spoon the cookie batter into six portions onto that baking sheet, giving them room to grow and expand.
- Add the cookies into the oven to bake for a little bit. You want to allow the bottoms to have time to brown as well.
- After about 6 to 8 minutes, the cookies should be done. Take them out of the oven and give them some time to cool before serving.

Nutrition:

Calories: 68

Total Fat: 1.8 g

Saturated Fat: 0.7 g

Cholesterol: 2 mg

69. Banana Pudding

Preparation Time: 10 minutes

Cooking Time: 15 minutes

Servings: 3

Ingredients:

- 1 sliced and peeled banana
- ½ tsp. Vanilla
- 1 c. Nonfat milk
- 2 tbsps. Cornstarch
- ¼ c. Sugar

Directions:

- Bring out a smaller bowl to start, and add the cornstarch and the sugar. Make sure to mix around to combine.
- Then it is time to bring out a small pan and add the milk. Turn on the heat on the stove and let it simmer for a bit, stirring the whole time.
- When the milk is nice and hot, pour your sugar and cornstarch mixture into this, making sure to whisk constantly the whole time.
- Cook this for another 5 minutes, stirring the mixture constantly. You know it is done when the mixture starts to coat the back of your spoon.
- After this time, take the pan off the heat and whisk in your vanilla. Divide up the slices of banana that you did before among four ramekins.
- Pour the pudding on top as evenly as you can. Then add to the fridge to cool down before you serve.

Nutrition:

Calories: 59

Total Fat: 1.8 g

Saturated Fat: 0.7 g

Cholesterol: 2 mg

70.Blueberry Cherry Crisp

Preparation Time: 5 minutes

Cooking Time: 35 minutes

Servings: 8

Ingredients:

- 1 c. old-fashioned oatmeal
- ⅓ c. coconut flour
- ½ c. chopped macadamia nuts
- 2 tbsps. coconut oil
- 3 tbsps. almond butter
- 2 tbsps. honey
- 1 tsp. Cinnamon
- ¼ tsp. Nutmeg
- ⅛ tsp. sea salt
- 4 c. frozen cherries, thawed
- 2 c. frozen blueberries

Directions:

- Set the oven to 375F. Almond butter in a 9x9 inch glass dish.
- Mix oatmeal with nuts and flour in a glass bowl.
- Heat honey with almond butter, coconut oil, nutmeg, sea salt, and cinnamon in a pan.
- Cook for 3 minutes on low heat while stirring.
- Gradually stir in the oatmeal mixture and keep mixing well.
- Spread the blueberries and cherries in the glass dish.
- Add the oatmeal mixture to the dish and spread it evenly.
- Bake for 35 minutes until bubbly.
- Serve,

Nutrition: Calories: 252 , Total Fat: 16 g , Saturated Fat: 7 g , Cholesterol: 11 mg , Sodium: 8 mg , Carbs: 29 g , Sugar: 1.8 g , Fiber: 5 g , Protein: 4 g

71. Baked Apples with Tahini Raisin Filling

Preparation Time: 10 minutes

Cooking Time: 35 minutes

Servings: 4

Ingredients:

- 4 ripe apples, cored
- ¾ c. tahini
- 1 c. apple juice
- 3 tbsps. raisins
- ⅓ c. chopped pecans
- ¼ tsp. cinnamon
- Dash of nutmeg
- Dash of vanilla
- ¾ c. boiling water

Directions:

- Set the oven to 375F to preheat. Grease a 9x13-inch baking dish with oil.
- Place the cored apples in the shallow dish.
- Mix tahini with half a cup of apple juice in a small bowl.
- Stir in pecans, raisins, nutmeg, vanilla, and cinnamon. Mix well.
- Stuff this mixture into the core of the apples.
- Add some boiling water to the baking dish.
- Pour the remaining apple juice on top.
- Bake for 35 minutes until tender.
- Serve the apples with the remaining juices on top.

Nutrition:

Calories: 386

Total Fat: 24 g

Saturated Fat: 3 g

Cholesterol: 0 mg

Sodium: 19 mg

Carbs: 41 g

Sugar: 1.9 g

Fiber: 7 g

Protein: 8 g

72. Vanilla Parfait

Preparation Time: 10 minutes

Cooking Time: 0 minutes

Servings: 2

Ingredients:

- 1 c. vanilla milk (unsweetened)
- 1 c. Greek yogurt (plain low-fat)
- 2 tbsps. agave
- 1 tsp. Vanilla
- ⅛ tsp. kosher salt
- ¼ c. chia seeds
- 2 c. sliced strawberries
- ¼ c. sliced almonds
- 4 tsp. agave for serving

Directions:

- Mix milk, yogurt, agave, vanilla, and salt in a medium bowl.
- Whisk in chia seeds and let them rest for 25 minutes.
- Cover the bowl and refrigerate it overnight.
- Mix strawberries with agave and toasted almonds in a bowl.
- Layer the serving glasses with yogurt pudding and strawberries alternatively.
- Serve.

Nutrition: Calories: 199 , Total Fat: 7g , Saturated Fat: 3.5 g , Cholesterol: 125 mg , Carbs: 7.2 g , Sugar: 1.4 g , Fiber: 2.1 g , Sodium: 135 mg. Protein: 4.7 g

73.Pumpkin Pudding Parfaits

Preparation Time: 10 minutes

Cooking Time: 22 minutes

Total time: 32 minutes

Servings: 6

Ingredients:

- 1 c. pumpkin puree
- ¼ c. packed Splenda
- ½ tsp. ground cinnamon
- 3 c. almond milk
- 2 tbsps. almond butter
- ½ c. Splenda
- 3 tbsps. xanthan gum
- 1 tsp. salt
- 4 large egg whites
- 2 tsp. vanilla extract

Directions:

- Mix pumpkin puree with cinnamon and Splenda in a saucepan.
- Stir and cook the mixture for 10 minutes until smooth.
- Heat 2 cups of milk with almond butter in a microwave for 2 minutes on high heat.
- Whisk Splenda with salt and xanthan gum in a large pan.
- Stir in 1 cup milk and mix well until smooth.
- Cook until the mixture thickens.
- Stir in vanilla and strain the mixture.
- Add half of the vanilla pudding to the pumpkin mixture.
- Mix well and divide the pumpkin pudding into serving cups.
- Top the pumpkin pudding with the remaining vanilla pudding.
- Refrigerate for 4 hours.
- Garnish as desired and serve.

Nutrition: Calories: 151 , Total Fat: 3.4 g , Saturated Fat: 7 g , Cholesterol: 20 mg , Carbs: 6.4 g , Sugar: 2.1 g , Fiber: 4.8 g , Sodium: 136 mg , Protein: 4.2 g

74. Banana Pudding Parfaits

Preparation Time: 10 minutes

Cooking Time: 15 minutes

Servings: 2

Ingredients:

- 1 c. Splenda
- ¼ c. xanthan gum
- ¼ tsp. salt
- 2 ½ c. almond milk
- 4 large egg whites
- 2 tbsps. unsalted almond butter
- 1 tsp. pure vanilla extract
- 2 bananas, sliced
- 12 shortbread cookies, crumbled

Directions:

- Mix Splenda with salt, xanthan gum, and milk in a saucepan.
- Stir cook until smooth, then whisk in egg whites.
- Cook until the mixture bubbles.
- Strain the mixture and stir in vanilla and almond butter. Mix well.
- Layer the serving glasses with slices of bananas, cookies, and pudding.
- Refrigerate for 1 hour.
- Serve.

Nutrition: Calories: 165 , Total Fat: 3 g, Saturated Fat: 0.2 g , Cholesterol: 09 mg , Sodium: 7.1 mg , Carbs: 17.5 g , Sugar: 1.1 g , Fiber: 0.5 g , Protein: 2.2 g

75.Oatmeal Cookies

Preparation Time: 5 minutes

Cooking Time: 10 minutes

Servings: 6

Ingredients:

- 1 c. coconut flour
- 1 c. quick-cooking oats
- ½ c. Splenda
- ½ tsp. Baking powder
- ½ tsp. Baking soda
- ½ tsp. Salt
- ½ tsp. ground cinnamon
- 2 egg whites
- ⅓ c. corn syrup
- 1 tsp. vanilla extract
- ⅓ c. raisins

Directions:

- Mix flour with oats, baking powder, soda, salt, cinnamon, and Splenda in a bowl.
- Fold in raisins and mix gently.
- Drop the batter on the baking sheet spoon by spoon.
- Bake at 375F in the preheated oven for 10 mins.
- Serve.

Nutrition:

Calories: 102

Total Fat: 1 g

Saturated Fat: 0 g

Cholesterol: 0 mg

Sodium: 138 mg

Carbs: 24 g

Fiber: 0g

Sugar: 0 g

Protein: 2 g

76.Gingersnaps

Preparation Time: 10 minutes

Cooking Time: 8 minutes

Servings: 6

Ingredients:

- ½ c. unsulphured molasses
- 1 egg white
- 3 ½ c. coconut flour
- 1 tsp. Baking soda
- ½ tsp. salt
- 2 tsps. ground ginger
- 1 tsp. Cinnamon
- ½ tsp. Ground cloves
- ½ tsp. Ground nutmeg
- ½ tsp. Freshly ground black pepper

Directions:

- Whisk almond butter with Splenda in a bowl.
- Stir in molasses and egg white. Mix well until smooth.
- Combine flour with salt, spices, and baking soda in a mixing bowl.
- Stir in almond butter mixture and mix well on low speed.
- Divide the dough into two halves. Wrap the dough in a plastic sheet.
- Refrigerate it for 3 hours.
- Set the oven to 350F.
- Unwrap the dough and keep it on a floured surface.
- Roll the dough into ⅛ inch thick sheet.
- Cut small cookies using a cookie cutter.
- Set the cookies on a baking sheet lined with parchment paper.
- Bake for 8 minutes until golden brown.
- Serve.

Nutrition:

Calories: 209

Total Fat: 0.5 g

Saturated Fat: 11.7 g

Cholesterol: 58 mg

Sodium: 163 mg

Carbs: 19.9 g

Fiber: 1.5 g

Sugar: 0.3 g

Protein: 3.3 g

77.Coconut Biscotti

Preparation Time: 10 minutes

Cooking Time: 60 minutes

Servings: 6

Ingredients:

- 1 ½ c. coconut flour
- ¾ tsp. Baking powder
- ¼ tsp. Salt
- ¼ tsp. Baking soda
- ⅛ tsp. grated whole nutmeg
- ¾ c. Splenda
- 1 tsp. vanilla extract
- 2 egg whites
- 1 c. flaked sweetened coconut

Directions:

- Set the oven to 300F to preheat.
- Mix all the ingredients in an electric mixer to form a smooth dough.
- Knead the dough, then make 3-inch rolls out of this dough.
- Place the rolls on the baking sheet lined with parchment paper.
- Lightly press each roll and bake for 40 minutes at 300F.
- Allow them to cool, then diagonally slice the rolls.
- Bake for another 20 minutes.
- Serve.

Nutrition:

Calories: 237

Total Fat: 19.8 g

Saturated Fat: 1.4 g

Cholesterol: 10 mg

Sodium: 719 mg

Carbs: 55.1 g

Fiber: 0.9 g

Sugar: 1.4 g

Protein: 17.8 g

78. Cheesecake Mousse with Raspberries

Preparation Time: 10 minutes

Cooking Time: 8 minutes

Servings: 6

Ingredients:

- 1 c. light lemonade filling
- 1 can of 8 oz cream cheese at room temperature
- ¾ c. Splenda no-calorie sweetener pellets
- 1 tbsp. lemon zest
- 1 tbsp. vanilla extract
- 1 c. fresh or frozen raspberries

Directions:

- Beat the cream cheese until it is sparkling; add ½ cup Splenda® Granules and mix until melted. Stir in lemon zest and vanilla.
- Reserve some raspberries for decoration. Crush the rest of the raspberries with a fork and mix them with ¼ cup Splenda pellets until they are melted.
- Lightly add the lump and cheese filling and then gently but quickly add crushed raspberries. Share this mousse in 6 ramekins with a spoon and keep in the refrigerator until tasting.
- Garnish mousses with reserved raspberries and garnish with fresh mint before serving.

Nutrition:

Calories: 259kcal

Carbs: 37g

Protein: 5g

Fat: 11g

Saturated Fat: 1g

Sodium: 197mg

79.Avocado Pudding

Preparation Time: 15 minutes

Cooking Time: 3¼ hours

Servings: 4

Ingredients:

- 2 c. bananas, peeled and chopped
- 2 ripe avocados, peeled, pitted, and chopped
- 1 tsp. fresh lime zest, grated finely
- 1 tsp. fresh lemon zest, grated finely
- ½ c. fresh lime juice
- ½ c. fresh lemon juice
- ⅓ c. agave nectar

Directions:

- In a blender, add all the ingredients and pulse until smooth.
- Transfer the mousse into four serving glasses and refrigerate to chill for about 3 hours before serving.

Nutrition:

Calories: 462
Total Fat: 20.1 g
Saturated Fat: 4.4 g
Cholesterol: 0 mg
Sodium: 13 mg
Carbs: 48.2 g
Fiber: 10.2 g
Sugar: 30.4 g
Protein: 3 g

80. Apple Crisp

Preparation Time: 15 minutes

Cooking Time: 20 minutes

Servings: 8

Ingredients:

For Filling:

- 2 large apples, peeled, cored, and chopped
- 2 tbsps. water
- 2 tbsps. Fresh apple juice
- ¼ tsp. ground cinnamon

For Topping:

- ½ c. quick rolled oats
- ¼ c. unsweetened coconut flakes
- 2 tbsps. Pecans, chopped
- ½ tsp. ground cinnamon
- ¼ c. water

Directions:

- Preheat the oven to 300F. Lightly grease a baking dish.
- To make the filling, add all the ingredients to a large bowl and gently mix. Set this aside.
- Make the topping by adding all the ingredients to another bowl and mixing well.
- Place the filling mixture into the prepared baking dish, then spread the topping over the filling mixture evenly.
- Bake for about 20 minutes or until the top becomes golden brown.
- Serve warm.

Nutrition:

Calories: 100

Total Fat: 2.7 g

Saturated Fat: 0.8 g

Cholesterol: 0 mg

Sodium: 3 mg

Carbs: 19.1 g

Fiber: 2.6 g

Sugar: 11.9 g

Protein: 1.2 g

CHAPTER 7:
Snacks

81.Blueberry Cherry Chip

Preparation Time: 15 minutes

Cooking Time: 40 minutes

Servings: 8

Ingredients:

- 1 c. oatmeal
- ⅓ c. whole wheat flour
- ½ c. macadamia nuts
- 2 tbsps. coconut oil
- 3 tbsps. butter
- 2 tbsps. honey
- 1 tsp. cinnamon
- ¼ tsp. nutmeg
- ⅛ tsp. salt
- 4 c. cherry frozen
- 2 c. blueberries, frozen

Directions:

- First, preheat the oven to 375F, and set the baking dish by greasing it with butter.
- Add oatmeal, flour, and nuts, and mix well.
- Add coconut oil, butter, honey, cinnamon, nutmeg, and salt to a pan. Stir the mixture on low flame until the butter melts and the mixture is well combined. Cook it for 3 minutes.
- After that, pour it into the oatmeal mixture and stir well. Set the berries and cherries in a dish and pour the mixture over them with a spoon.
- Bake them for 35 to 40 minutes or until crispy. Serve when cool down.

Nutrition:

Calories: 140

Total Fat: 4 g

Saturated Fat: 0.5 g

Fiber: 1.2 g

Sugar: 1 g

82. Baked Apple with Tahini Raisin Filling

Preparation Time: 15 minutes

Cooking Time: 30 minutes

Servings: 4

Ingredients:

- 4 apples
- ¾ c. tahini
- 1 c. apple juice
- 3 tbsps. raisins
- ⅓ c. pecans
- ¼ tsp. cinnamon
- Nutmeg as per taste
- Vanilla as per taste
- ¾ c. water boiling

Directions:

- Set the baking dish with oil grease and heat the oven to 375F.
- Cut the apples from the center to remove the core and set them in a baking dish.
- Add tahini, apple juice, cinnamon, nutmeg, and vanilla to a small bowl, and mix them.
- Now fill the center core of the apples with the mixture.
- Pour the boiling water in a baking dish and apple juice over the apples and bake for 30 minutes.
- After that, remove from the oven and serve warm.

Nutrition:

Calories: 125

Total Fat: 4 g

Saturated Fat: 0.5 g

Fiber: 1.2 g

Sugar: 1 g

83.Berry Banana Slush

Preparation Time: 5 minutes

Cooking Time: 5 minutes

Servings: 2

Ingredients:

- 2 bananas
- 200 g frozen berries
- Ice cubes, if required

Directions:

- Take a blender and pour the mixed berries inside, including blueberries, strawberries, and raspberries and blend them well until they turn into a combined slush. Add ice if you'd like to increase the slushy consistency.
- In serving cups, add the banana cubes, and pour the berry slush on them. Serve the chill and yummy banana berry slush.

Nutrition:

Calories: 122

Total Fat: 4 g

Saturated Fat: 0.5 g

Fiber: 1.2 g

Sugar: 1 g

84.Sticky Toffee Pudding

Preparation Time: 25 minutes

Cooking Time: 1 hour

Servings: 4

Ingredients:

- 175 g dates, dried
- 150 ml maple syrup
- 1 tbsp. vanilla extract
- 2 eggs
- 85g flour

Directions:

- Preheat the oven to 180C.
- Take a pan, add water and pour dates. Cook on low flame for 5 to 6 minutes.
- Add the dates and water into the blender and pulse until they turn smooth. Add maple syrup and vanilla extract and blend again.
- Pour the mixture into a bowl. Now whisk the egg into a separate bowl.
- In the dates mixture, add flour and egg and fold them well until well combined. Take a pudding pan and pour maple syrup into the base. Pour the mixture on it and bake for at least an hour.
- After that, transfer it to the serving plate, dress it with maple syrup, and serve.

Nutrition:

Calories: 111

Total Fat: 4 g

Saturated Fat: 0.5 g

Fiber: 1.2 g

Sugar: 1 g

85.Lighter Apple & Pear Pie

Preparation Time: 20 minutes

Cooking Time: 40 minutes

Servings: 6

Ingredients:

- 6 apples
- 4 pears
- 1 lemon juice & zest
- 3 tbsps. syrup
- 1 tsp. mixed spice
- 1 tbsp. corn flour
- 4 pastry sheets
- 4 tsp. rapeseed oil
- 25g almond

Directions:

- Take a pan, add apples and pears with water, syrup, lemon, and mixed spices, and cook for 5 minutes.
- Remove the fruit, pour it into a pie dish, and cook the remainder for another 5 minutes.
- Mash the remaining fruits into a mixer until smooth and until the syrup is thick in consistency. Cook that syrup for another 4 to 5 minutes, and then pour it into a pie dish.
- Set the pastry sheets in the dish and brush oil on the top. Bake it for 30 minutes in a preheated oven at 180C until it turns brown and is cooked. Serve immediately!

Nutrition:

Calories: 175

Total Fat: 4 g

Saturated Fat: 0.5 g

Fiber: 1.2 g

Sugar: 1 g

86. Peach & Blueberry Yogurt Cake

Preparation Time: 20 minutes

Cooking Time: 1 hour

Servings: 10

Ingredients:

- 1 ½ c. all-purpose flour
- 1 tsp. Baking powder
- ½ tsp. baking soda
- 2 oz. butter
- 1 c. sugar
- 2 eggs
- ½ tsp. vanilla
- ½ c. yogurt
- 2 peaches, sliced
- 6 oz. blueberries
- 1 tsp. sugar

Directions:

- Grease the baking pan with parchment paper and set aside.
- Preheat the oven to 350F.
- Take a bowl, and add flour, baking powder, and soda. Whisk eggs, butter, and sugar in a separate bowl until fluffy.
- Now add vanilla extract and Greek yogurt and continue beating until well combined and the texture becomes smooth. Pour the mixture into a flour bowl and mix until well combined.
- Pour the batter into the baking pan, set the slices of peach, and sprinkle blueberries with sugar. Bake it for 30 to 35 minutes or until golden brown.
- After baking, let it cool down for 30 minutes and serve with the yogurt topping.

Nutrition:

Calories: 202

Total Fat: 4 g

Saturated Fat: 0.5 g

Fiber: 1.2 g

Sugar: 1 g

87.Dark Chocolate Cheese Bar

Preparation Time: 15 minutes

Cooking Time: 1 hour

Servings: 12

Ingredients:

- 1 c. cracker crumbs
- ¼ c. coconut flour
- ¼ c. cocoa powder
- 8 tbsps. cream cheese
- 2 tbsps. honey
- 1 tsp. vanilla extract
- 2 to 3 tbsps. almond milk
- ⅓ c. dark chocolate chips
- 1 tsp. coconut oil

Directions:

- Set up a tray with the parchment paper and set it aside.
- Add graham cracker crumbs, coconut flour, and cocoa powder to a bowl and add them into a mixture. Then pour honey, vanilla extract, and cream cheese.
- Mix them well to turn them into a fine dough.
- Gradually add the almond milk to make the dough soft, and do not let it dry. When it's done, set it into a baking pan with the help of a spatula.
- Add chocolate chips and coconut oil to a small bowl and set it in the microwave until melted and smooth. Pour the chocolate over the batter and set it evenly.
- Now put the tray into the fridge for some time until the ingredients set well.
- Serve the fine dark chocolate cheese bar.

Nutrition: Calories: 140 , Total Fat: 4 g , Saturated Fat: 0.5 g , Fiber: 1.2 g , Sugar: 1 g

88. Green Yogurt Kick

Preparation Time: 10 minutes

Cooking Time: 0 minutes

Servings: 1

Ingredients:

- ½ Gala Apple
- ½ c. Spinach
- ½ Banana
- ¾ c. Yogurt
- ¼ c. cubed Papaya

Directions:

- Peel and core the apple and then chop it into smaller pieces.
- Place the apple and the other ingredients in the bowl of your blender.
- Blend for a minute or until smooth.
- Serve immediately and enjoy.

Nutrition:

Calories: 150

Fat: 8

Fiber: 2

Carbs: 4

Protein: 9

89.Skinny Chocolate Chip Cheesecake Bar

Preparation Time: 15 minutes

Cooking Time: 35 minutes

Servings: 16

Ingredients:

- ¾ c. graham cracker crumbs
- 2 tbsps. butter
- 8 oz. cream cheese
- ¾ c. Greek yogurt
- 2 eggs
- ¼ c. sugar
- 2 tbsps. flour
- 1 tbsp. lemon juice
- 2 tbsps. vanilla extract
- ½ c. chocolate chips

Directions:

- Preheat the oven to 350F and set the baking tray aside by setting parchment paper.
- In a blender, add cracker crumbs and pour butter to blend well.
- Transfer the mixture to a baking tray, set it with a spatula, and bake for 8 to 10 minutes.
- In a mixer, add cream cheese and beat for a minute. Add yogurt, egg, sugar, and flour and mix until smooth. Add the lemon juice and mix well.
- Now pour the mixture into a bowl, add chocolate chips, and fold them well. Cover the baked crust with the cream cheese filling and bake for 20 to 25 minutes until cooked.
- After that, let it cool down and serve it hot or chilled.

Nutrition:

Calories: 140

Total Fat: 4 g

Saturated Fat: 0.5 g

Fiber: 1.2 g

Sugar: 1 g

90. Frozen Fruit Skewers

Preparation Time: 30 minutes

Cooking Time: 0

Servings: 12

Ingredients:

- ¼ of watermelon, cubed
- ½ cantaloupe, cubed
- ½ pineapple, cubed
- 1 c. grapes
- 6 oz. blueberries
- 2 to 3 bananas, sliced
- 4 oz. chocolate chips

Directions:

- Take the fruits and cut them in evenly into cubes.
- Thread the fruit alternatively on the skewers. Cover the skewers with a plastic sheet and put them in the refrigerator until ready to serve.
- In a bowl, add chocolate chips and melt in a microwave for 2 to 3 minutes until smooth. Let the chocolate cool down a bit.
- Remove the fruit skewers and drizzle the melted chocolate over the fruit skewers.
- Now put it into the refrigerator and let it freeze. Serve frozen fruit skewer immediately!

Nutrition:

Calories: 121

Total Fat: 4 g

Saturated Fat: 0.5 g

Fiber: 1.2 g

Sugar: 1 g

91. Whole Wheat Chocolate Cake Donuts

Preparation Time: 5 minutes

Cooking Time: 15 minutes

Servings: 6

Ingredients:

- ¾ c. almond milk
- 1 tsp. lemon juice
- 1 c. whole wheat flour
- 2 tbsps. sugar
- 2 tsp. Cocoa powder
- ½ tsp. Baking powder
- ½ tsp. Baking soda
- ½ tsp. Salt
- ½ tbsp. flax seed
- 2 tbsps. oil
- 1 c. sugar, powdered
- 1 tsp. vanilla extract
- 1 tbsp. milk

Directions:

- Preheat the oven to 350F and set the doughnut baking tray. Mix the almond milk with lemon juice in a small bowl and set aside for 5 minutes. Add flour, flaxseed, sugar, cocoa powder, baking powder, baking soda, salt, and oil to a bowl, and mix them well. Now pour the almond milk and lemon mixture into it until combined. Pour the batter over the doughnut baking tray and bake for 10 to 13 minutes or until fluffy and cooked. Remove them and let them cool down. Sprinkle powdered sugar or milk.

Nutrition:

Calories: 175

Total Fat: 4 g

Saturated Fat: 0.5 g

Fiber: 1.2 g

Sugar: 1 g

92.Blueberry and Cream Dessert

Preparation Time: 30 minutes

Cooking Time: 15 minutes

Servings:

Ingredients:

- 12 oz. blueberries, frozen
- 2 tbsps. sugar
- 2 tbsps. cornstarch
- ¼ c. water
- 1 tbsp. lemon juice
- 16 oz. light cream cheese
- ⅔ c. dried milk
- ⅔ c. granulated sugar
- 1 ½ heavy cream
- 3 tbsps. powdered sugar

Directions:

- Add water, blueberries, sugar, cornstarch, and lemon juice. Bring it to a boil and simmer for 5 to 7 minutes over a medium flame. Let it cool down to room temperature. For the cake and cream layer, take a blender, add cream cheese, milk, and sugar and blend until smooth and creamy. Fold the cream cheese mixture with the cake cubes until well combined. Mix the heavy cream with the sugar for the whipped cream until it turns soft and fluffy. In a serving cup, fill it with the mixture, and add blueberry syrup and another layer of creamy cheesecake. After that, dress it in the whipped cream and put it in the refrigerator for 2 hours to set and chill it. Serve the chilled blueberry cream dessert.

Nutrition:

Calories: 143

Total Fat: 4 g

Saturated Fat: 0.5 g

Fiber: 1.2 g

Sugar: 1 g

93.Zucchini Hummus

Preparation Time: 15 minutes

Cooking Time: 20 minutes

Servings: 5

Ingredients:

- Salt
- ½ tsp. Grated lemon zest
- 1 tsp. Chopped dill, fresh
- 1 Tbsp. Tahini
- 1 Tbsp. Olive oil
- 1 Chopped zucchini

Directions:

- To start this recipe, bring out a food processor or a blender and set it up.
- When that is ready, add the salt, lemon zest, dill, tahini, olive oil, and zucchini to the mix and blend.
- When this is nice and smooth, you can pour the ingredients into a bowl and serve when ready.

Nutrition:

Calories: 93

Total Fat: 4 g

Saturated Fat: 0.5 g

Fiber: 1.2 g

Sugar: 1 g

94.Salmon Canapes

Preparation Time: 20 minutes

Cooking Time: 20 minutes

Servings: 6

Ingredients:

- 1 sliced zucchini in 12 rounds
- Salt
- 1 tsp. Tarragon, chopped
- 1 tsp. Orange zest, grated
- ¼ c. Plain yogurt
- 4 oz. Canned salmon

Directions:

- For this recipe, take out a bowl before combining the tarragon, salt, orange zest, yogurt, and salmon.
- When this is ready, lay out the zucchini rounds flatly. Add the salmon mixture on top of the zucchini rounds and enjoy it.

Nutrition:

Calories: 64

Total Fat: 4 g

Saturated Fat: 0.5 g

Fiber: 1.2 g

Sugar: 1 g

95.Sweet Potato Fries

Preparation Time: 15 minutes

Cooking Time: 25 minutes

Servings: 7

Ingredients:

- 1 sliced sweet potato
- 1 Tbsp. Olive oil
- ½ tsp. Salt
- 1 tsp. Ground cumin

Directions:

- Turn on the oven and give it time to heat up to 450F.
- While the oven is heating up, take out a bowl so you can toss together the olive oil, salt, cumin, and sweet potato sticks.
- When combined well, you can pour them onto a baking sheet with a rim. Make sure that it is all in a single layer.
- Add the baking sheet with the ingredients into the oven and let them bake. You will need to keep a spatula on hand to flip these around to cook evenly halfway through the process.
- After 20 minutes or so, the sweet potato fries should be done. You can take them out of the oven before serving.

Nutrition:

Calories: 87

Total Fat: 4 g

Saturated Fat: 0.5 g

Fiber: 1.2 g

Sugar: 1 g

96. Mashed Potatoes

Preparation Time: 10 minutes

Cooking Time: 15 minutes

Servings: 4

Ingredients:

- Salt
- 2 tbsps. Butter
- ½ c. Nonfat milk
- 2 cubed and peeled russet potatoes

Directions:

- When you are ready to start this, take out a pot and add the potatoes inside of it. Cover them with just enough water to get all around the potatoes.
- Add the lid to the pot and then cook the potatoes on high heat until the potatoes have time to become soft.
- After about fifteen minutes, we can take the potatoes from the heat and drain the water. Ensure the potatoes return to the pot when you are done draining.
- This is where we add in the salt, butter, and milk. Use a potato masher to mash everything together until smooth.
- Take a test and see if there needs to be more seasoning before serving.

Nutrition:

Calories: 54

Total Fat: 4 g

Saturated Fat: 0.5 g

Fiber: 1.2 g

Sugar: 1 g

97. Melony Probiotic

Preparation Time: 5 minutes

Cooking Time: 0 minutes

Servings: 2

Ingredients:

- 1 c. Kefir
- 1 c. Melon Chunks
- 1 tsp. minced Ginger
- A handful of watercress
- ½ cucumber

Directions:

- Peel and chop the cucumber and place it in your blender along with the remaining Ingredients.
- Blend until the mixture becomes smooth.
- Serve immediately and enjoy!

Nutrition:

Calories: 170

Fat: 17.8

Fiber: 1.5

Carbs: 3.8

Protein: 1.5

98. Quinoa Pilaf

Preparation Time: 10 minutes

Cooking Time: 20 minutes

Servings: 5

Ingredients:

- ½ tsp. Salt
- 2 tbsps. Chopped parsley
- 2 tbsps. Raisins
- ¼ c. Pine nuts
- 1 c. Vegetable broth
- ½ c. Rinsed quinoa
- 1 chopped and peeled carrots

Directions:

- To start, take out a pot and heat it over the stove. Add in the broth and the carrot, and then cook. You will want to stir this as you go and wait a few minutes until the carrot has time to brown.
- When this time is up, add in the quinoa and the rest of the broth. Reduce the heat to a simmer and cover the pot to cook the quinoa.
- It will take around 15 minutes for the quinoa to cook through. When this is done, add salt, parsley, raisins, and pine nuts before you serve and enjoy.

Nutrition:

Calories: 77

Total Fat: 4 g

Saturated Fat: 0.5 g

Fiber: 1.2 g

Sugar: 1 g

99. Yummy Vanilla Parfait

Preparation Time: 10 minutes

Cooking Time: 20 minutes

Servings: 3

Ingredients:

- 4 tsp. Agave
- 1 c. Vanilla milk
- 2 c. Figs, sliced
- Salt
- 2 tbsps. Agave
- ¼ c. Chia seeds
- 1 tsp. Vanilla
- 1 c. yogurt, Greek
- ¼ c. Almonds, sliced

Directions:

- To start this recipe, take out a medium bowl and mix the salt, vanilla, agave, yogurt, and milk until they are well combined.
- When that is done, whisk in the chia seeds. Set the bowl aside and let it rest for a bit. Twenty-five minutes should be enough for this one.
- When that time is up, cover up the bowl and set it in the fridge. Make sure to let it stay there overnight.
- The following morning mix in the toasted almonds, agave, and figs in the bowl. Layer the mixture into the serving glasses and enjoy right away.

Nutrition:

Calories: 86

Total Fat: 4 g

Saturated Fat: 0.5 g

Fiber: 1.2 g

Sugar: 1 g

100.　Nut Bag

Preparation Time: 10 minutes

Cooking Time: 20 minutes

Servings: 5

Ingredients:

- 1 tsp. Salt
- 1 tsp. Olive oil
- 1 oz. Brazil nuts
- 1 oz. Almonds

Directions:

- Turn on the oven and let it heat up to 365F. While the oven is warming up, crush the Brazil nuts and the almonds gently before sprinkling on some salt.
- When the oven is ready, take the nuts and add them to a tray, stirring around in some olive oil simultaneously.
- Add the tray into the oven and then cook for a bit. After 8 minutes, the nuts should be done, and you can take them out of the oven.
- Allow these to chill until they get to room temperature, and then move them to a paper bag before serving.

Nutrition:

Calories: 54
Total Fat: 4 g
Saturated Fat: 0.5 g
Fiber: 1.2 g
Sugar: 1 g

CHAPTER 8:
Smoothies

101. Avocado and Frozen Banana Smoothie

Preparation Time: 10 minutes

Cooking Time: 0 minutes

Servings: 1

Ingredients:

- 1 ½ frozen bananas
- 1 avocado
- ½ c. red grapes
- 2 tbsps. ground almonds
- 1 ¼ c. almond milk
- A pinch of cinnamon

Directions:

- Peel the avocado and remove the pit.
- Place it in the bowl of your blender along with the other Ingredients.
- Blend until smooth, about a minute or two.
- Serve immediately and enjoy!

Nutrition:

Calories: 93

Fat: 1.8

Fiber: 10.6

Carbs: 18.6

Protein: 3.4

102. Peachy and Gingery Balancer

Preparation Time: 5 minutes

Cooking Time: 0 minutes

Servings: 1

Ingredients:

- 1 peach, chopped
- ½ c. yogurt
- ¼ tsp. grated ginger
- 1 tbsp. maple syrup
- ½ apple (make sure to use sweet apples only as sour ones can aggravate your sensitive gut)

Directions:

- Peel, core, and chop the apple.
- Place it in the bowl of your blender along with the remaining Ingredients.
- Blend until smooth.
- Serve immediately and enjoy!

Nutrition:

Calories: 258

Fat: 21.8

Fiber: 4.9

Carbs: 11.9

Protein: 6.6

103. Banana Peanut Butter Smoothie

Preparation Time: 5 minutes

Cooking Time: 0 minutes

Servings: 1

Ingredients:

- 2 tbsps. Peanut Butter
- 2 bananas
- 1 sweet apple
- ⅔ c. Milk
- ¼ tsp. Vanilla Extract

Directions:

- Peel, core, and chop the apple.
- Place it in the bowl of your blender along with the remaining Ingredients.
- Blend until smooth.
- Pour into two glasses and enjoy!

Nutrition:

Calories: 300

Fat: 4

Fiber: 4

Carbs: 10

Protein: 7

104. Green Weapon

Preparation Time: 5 minutes

Cooking Time: 0 minutes

Servings: 1

Ingredients:

- ½ c. Baby Spinach
- 2 Kale Leaves, chopped
- A handful of Watercress
- 1 Mango, chopped
- ½ c. Coconut Water
- ½ Sweet Apple

Directions:

- Peel, core, and chop the apple.
- Place it in your blender along with the remaining Ingredients.
- Blend until the mixture becomes smooth.
- Serve immediately and enjoy!

Nutrition:

Calories: 270

Fat: 4

Fiber: 6

Carbs: 8

Protein: 12

105. Almond Butter Smoothie

Preparation Time: 5 minutes

Cooking Time: 0 minutes

Servings: 1

Ingredients:

- ½ c. Almond Milk
- 1 tbsp. Almond Butter
- ½ Avocado
- 1 Pear
- Pinch of Cinnamon

Directions:

- Peel, core, and chop the pear.
- Place it in your blender along with the remaining Ingredients.
- Blend for a minute or until smooth.
- Serve immediately and enjoy!

Nutrition:

Calories: 340

Fat: 5

Fiber: 7

Carbs: 13

Protein: 15

106. Apple Ginger Smoothie

Preparation Time: 10 minutes

Cooking Time: 0 minutes

Servings: 1

Ingredients:

- 1 Apple, peeled and diced
- ¾ c. (6 oz.) coconut yogurt
- ½ tsp. Ginger, freshly grated

Directions:

- Add all the ingredients to a blender.
- Blend well until smooth.
- Refrigerate for 2 to 3 hours.
- Serve.

Nutrition:

Calories: 144

Total Fat: 0.4 g

Saturated Fat: 5 g

Cholesterol: 51 mg

Sodium: 86 mg

Carbs: 8 g

Fiber: 2.3 g

Sugar: 2.2 g

Protein: 5.6 g

107. Green Tea Blueberry Smoothie

Preparation Time: 10 minutes

Cooking Time: 5 minutes

Servings: 1

Ingredients:

- 3 tbsps. alkaline water
- 1 green tea bag
- 1½ c. fresh blueberries
- 1 pear, peeled, cored, and diced
- ¾ c. almond milk

Directions:

- Boil three tablespoons of water in a small pot and transfer it to a cup.
- Dip the tea bag in the cup and let it sit for 4 to 5 mins.
- Discard tea bag and
- Transfer the green tea to a blender
- Add all the remaining ingredients to the blender.
- Blend well until smooth.
- Serve with fresh blueberries.

Nutrition:

Calories: 144

Total Fat: 0.4 g

Saturated Fat: 5 g

Cholesterol: 51 mg

Sodium: 86 mg

Carbs: 8 g

Fiber: 2.3 g

Sugar: 2.2 g

Protein: 5.6 g

108. Apple Almond Smoothie

Preparation Time: 10 minutes

Cooking Time: 0 minutes

Servings: 1

Ingredients:

- 1 c. apple cider
- ½ c. coconut yogurt
- 4 tbsps. Almonds, crushed
- ¼ tsp. Cinnamon
- ¼ tsp. nutmeg
- 1 c. ice cubes

Directions:

- Add all the ingredients to a blender.
- Blend well until smooth.
- Serve.

Nutrition:

Calories: 144

Total Fat: 0.4 g

Saturated Fat: 5 g

Cholesterol: 51 mg

Sodium: 86 mg

Carbs: 8 g

Fiber: 2.3 g

Sugar: 2.2 g

Protein: 5.6 g

109.   Cranberry Smoothie

Preparation Time: 10 minutes

Cooking Time: 0 minutes

Servings: 1

Ingredients:

- 1 c. cranberries
- ¾ c. almond milk
- ¼ c. raspberries
- 2 tsp. fresh ginger, finely grated
- 2 tsps. Fresh lemon juice

Directions:

- Add all the ingredients to a blender.
- Blend well until smooth.
- Serve with fresh berries on top.

Nutrition:

Calories: 144
Total Fat: 0.4 g
Saturated Fat: 5 g
Cholesterol: 51 mg
Sodium: 86 mg
Carbs: 8 g
Fiber: 2.3 g
Sugar: 2.2 g
Protein: 5.6 g

110.   Cinnamon Berry Smoothie

Preparation Time: 10 minutes

Cooking Time: 0 minutes

Servings: 1

Ingredients:

- 1 c. frozen strawberries
- 1 c. apple, peeled and diced
- 2 tsp. fresh ginger
- 3 tbsps. hemp seeds
- 1 c. water
- ½ lime juiced
- ¼ tsp. Cinnamon powder
- ⅛ tsp. vanilla extract

Directions:

- Add all the ingredients to a blender.
- Blend well until smooth.
- Serve with fresh fruits

Nutrition:

Calories: 144

Total Fat: 0.4 g

Saturated Fat: 5 g

Cholesterol: 51 mg

Sodium: 86 mg

Carbs: 8 g

Fiber: 2.3 g

Sugar: 2.2 g

Protein: 5.6 g

111. Detox Berries Smoothie

Preparation Time: 10 minutes

Cooking Time: 0 minutes

Servings: 1

Ingredients:

- 3 peaches, cored and peeled
- 5 blueberries
- 5 raspberries
- 1 c. alkaline water

Directions:

- Add all the ingredients to a blender.
- Blend well until smooth.
- Serve with fresh kiwi wedges.

Nutrition:

Calories: 144
Total Fat: 0.4 g
Saturated Fat: 5 g
Cholesterol: 51 mg
Sodium: 86 mg
Carbs: 8 g
Fiber: 2.3 g
Sugar: 2.2 g
Protein: 5.6 g

112. Pink Smoothie

Preparation Time: 10 minutes

Cooking Time: 0 minutes

Servings: 1

Ingredients:

- 1 peach, cored and peeled
- 6 ripe strawberries
- 1 c. almond milk

Directions:

- Add all the ingredients to a blender.
- Blend well until smooth.
- Serve with your favorite berries

Nutrition:

Calories: 144

Total Fat: 0.4 g

Saturated Fat: 5 g

Cholesterol: 51 mg

Sodium: 86 mg

Carbs: 8 g

Fiber: 2.3 g

Sugar: 2.2 g

Protein: 5.6 g

113. Green Apple Smoothie

Preparation Time: 10 minutes

Cooking Time: 0 minutes

Servings: 1

Ingredients:

- 1 peach, peeled and cored
- 1 green apple, peeled and cored
- 1 c. alkaline water

Directions:

- Add all the ingredients to a blender.
- Blend well until smooth.
- Serve with apple slices.

Nutrition:

Calories: 144
Total Fat: 0.4 g
Saturated Fat: 5 g
Cholesterol: 51 mg
Sodium: 86 mg
Carbs: 8 g
Fiber: 2.3 g
Sugar: 2.2 g
Protein: 5.6 g

114. Avocado Smoothie

Preparation Time: 10 minutes

Cooking Time: 0 minutes

Servings: 1

Ingredients:

- 1 carrot, grated
- One avocado, cored and peeled
- ½ pear, cored
- ½ c. blackberries
- 1 ½ c. unsweetened almond milk

Directions:

- Add all the ingredients to a blender.
- Blend well until smooth.
- Serve with blackberries on top.

Nutrition:

Calories: 144

Total Fat: 0.4 g

Saturated Fat: 5 g

Cholesterol: 51 mg

Sodium: 86 mg

Carbs: 8 g

Fiber: 2.3 g

Sugar: 2.2 g

Protein: 5.6 g

115. Green Smoothie

Preparation Time: 10 minutes

Cooking Time: 0 minutes

Servings: 1

Ingredients:

- 1 c. alkaline water
- ¾ c. raw coconut water
- ½ tsp. probiotic powder
- 2 c. firmly packed baby spinach
- 1 c. raw young Thai coconut meat
- 1 avocado, peeled and pitted
- ½ cucumber, chopped
- 1 tsp. lime zest, finely grated
- 2 limes
- Stevia, to taste
- A pinch of Celtic sea salt
- 2 c. ice cubes

Directions:

- Add all the ingredients to a blender.
- Blend well until smooth.
- Serve with an avocado slice on top.

Nutrition:

Calories: 144

Total Fat: 0.4 g

Saturated Fat: 5 g

Cholesterol: 51 mg

Sodium: 86 mg

Carbs: 8 g

Fiber: 2.3 g

Sugar: 2.2 g

Protein: 5.6 g

116. Avocado and Kale Smoothie

This green smoothie is packed with lots of nutrition, like balanced, healthy omega fatty acids from the hemp seeds, healthy fat and Fiber from the avocado, and vitamins K and A from the kale. It's naturally sweetened with half a banana, so it's not overly sweet, but feel free to use the whole banana if you prefer your smoothie a little sweeter. The avocado is added for its nutritional benefits and also because it will give the smoothie a thicker and creamier texture. Any variety of kale will work—just make sure you stem it before adding it to your blender.

Preparation Time: 5 minutes

Cooking Time: 0

Servings: 2

Ingredients:

- 1½ c. almond milk
- 2 kale stalks, stemmed
- ½ avocado, roughly chopped
- ½ banana, roughly chopped
- 1 tbsp. hemp seeds

Directions:

- In a blender, combine almond milk, kale, avocado, banana, and hemp seeds until creamy and smooth.
- Pour into one large or two small glasses and enjoy.

Nutrition:

Calories: 200

Fat: 3

Fiber: 4

Carbs: 9

Protein: 10

117.   Hemp Seed and Banana Green Smoothie

Hemp seeds and almond butter are amazing plant-based proteins, adding about 17 grams of protein to the smoothie, and red chard is an amazing source of vitamins K, A, and C. Add the ice cubes if you like your smoothies cool and icy.

Preparation Time: 5 minutes

Cooking Time: 0 minutes

Servings: 2

Ingredients:

- 1½ c. coconut milk (boxed)
- ½ to 1 banana, roughly chopped
- ½ c. chopped rainbow or red chard
- 2 tbsps. almond butter
- 2 tbsps. hemp seeds
- 5 to 7 ice cubes (optional)

Directions:

- In a blender, blend to combine the coconut milk, banana, chard, almond butter, hemp seeds, and ice (if using) until creamy and smooth.
- Pour into one large or two small glasses and enjoy.

Nutrition:

Calories: 150

Fat: 3

Fiber: 7

Carbs: 15

Protein: 9

118.   Peach and Kale Protein Smoothie

Commercial protein powders are usually made with highly processed, unnecessary Ingredients. A complete protein with 19 grams of protein in one serving of pumpkin protein powder, made from 100% organic pumpkin seeds, is an easy and healthy way to add quality plant-based protein to your smoothies, desserts, and other snacks.

Preparation Time: 5 minutes

Cooking Time: 0

Servings: 1-2

Ingredients:

- 1½ c. coconut milk (boxed)
- 2 romaine lettuce leaves
- 1 kale stalk, stemmed
- 1 peach, roughly chopped
- ½ to 1 banana, roughly chopped
- 5 tbsps. pumpkin protein powder
- 5 to 7 ice cubes (optional)

Directions:

- In a blender, blend to combine the coconut milk, lettuce, kale, peach, banana, pumpkin protein powder, and ice (if using) until smooth.
- Pour into one large or two small glasses and enjoy.

Nutrition:

Calories: 300

Fat: 4

Fiber: 8

Carbs: 14

Protein: 13

119. Lemon-Ginger Green Smoothie

Lemon and ginger root imbue this smoothie with lots of antioxidant and anti-inflammatory goodness. Nutrient-dense greens, kale, and romaine lettuce give it its bright green color and essential vitamins K and A. Because ginger has a natural spicy (but delicious) bite, start with a small piece and add until the beverage tastes right.

Preparation Time: 5 minutes

Cooking Time: minutes

Servings: 1-2

Ingredients:

- 1½ c. coconut milk (boxed)
- 2 stalks of kale stemmed and roughly chopped
- 2 stalks of romaine lettuce, roughly chopped
- ½ celery stalk, roughly chopped
- 1 apple, cored and roughly chopped
- 1 tbsp. freshly squeezed lemon juice
- ¼- to ½-inch piece of ginger root, peeled and chopped
- 5 to 7 ice cubes (optional)

Directions:

- In a high-speed blender, blend to combine the coconut milk, kale, romaine, celery, apple, lemon juice, ginger, and ice (if using) until smooth.
- Pour into one large or two small glasses and enjoy.

Nutrition:

Calories: 200

Fat: 4

Fiber: 7

Carbs: 13

Protein: 16

120. Triple Berry Protein Smoothie

Berries are an excellent source of antioxidants, and this smoothie contains three different types of berries: raspberries, blueberries, and blackberries. Suppose you want to increase the nutritional benefits of this smoothie. In that case, you can use the smaller wild blueberries instead of the larger regular cultivated blueberries, as they contain twice the amount of antioxidants.

Preparation Time: 50 minutes

Cooking Time: 0

Servings: 1-2

Ingredients:

- 1½ c. coconut milk (boxed)
- ⅓ c. raspberries
- ⅓ c. blueberries
- ⅓ c. blackberries
- 3 tbsps. 100% pumpkin protein powder

Directions:

- In a blender, combine the coconut milk, raspberries, blueberries, blackberries, and pumpkin protein powder until well combined and smooth.

Nutrition:

Calories: 223

Fat: 3

Fiber: 7

Carbs: 10

Protein: 7

CHAPTER 9:
28-Day Meal Plan

Days	Breakfast	Lunch	Dinner	Dessert
1	Coconut Rice Pudding	Sweet & Sour Ground Chicken	Barbecued Rump Of Beef In Dijon	Almond Meringue Cookies
2	Oatmeal With Blueberries, Sunflower Seeds	Cuban Beef And Zucchini Kebabs	Grilled Chicken With Thyme	Yogurt And Melon Ice Pops
3	Baked Apples With Cinnamon & Ginger	White Bean, Chicken, And Rosemary Casserole	Marinated Lamb Steaks	Cinnamon Popcorn
4	Pear Banana Nut Muffins	Easy Turkey Meatloaf "Muffins"	Oat And Chickpea Dumplings	Baked Apples With Tahini Raisin Filling
5	Steel Cut Oatmeal	Thai Tofu And Red Cabbage Bowl	Rosemary Broiled Shrimp	Cheesecake Mousse With Raspberries
6	Corn Porridge With Maple And Raisins	Spaghetti With Watercress And Pea Pesto	Vegetarian Pasta Bakes With Halloumi	Pumpkin Pudding Parfaits
7	Omega- Overnight Oats	Chicken And Fennel Sauté	Broccoli Pesto Penne With Chili And Garlic	Oatmeal Cookies
8	Banana Breakfast Pudding	Vegan Vegetable Curry	Fritto Misto With Gremolata	Banana Pudding
9	Mango Salsa	Grilled Chicken & Spinach	Vegan Shepherd's Pie	Apple Crisp
10	English Muffins	Mediterranean Lamb Stew With Olives	Sautéed Chicken With Zucchini	Coconut Biscotti
11	Muesli-Style Oatmeal	Chicken With Kale	Brown Rice Chicken Salad	Carob And Peanut Butter Balls
12	Mexican Breakfast Toast	Beef Massaman Curry	Mushroom Risotto	Spiced Walnuts
13	Milky Oat	Turkey With Greens	Flank Steak	Peanut Butter Cookies
14	Quick Banana Sorbet	Pepper And Onion Tart	Lamb Kofta Curry	Baked Chips

15	Quinoa Porridge	Avocado Cream & Noodles	Roast Rib Of Beef	Banana Pudding Parfaits
16	Pumpkin Pancakes	Seafood Paella Recipe	Turkey Stew	Blueberry Cherry Crisp
17	Banana Bread	Herb And Spiced Lamb	Seafood Stew	Banana Dessert
18	Papaya Breakfast Boat	Veggie Rice Bowl	Fritto Misto	Vanilla Parfait
19	Kale Salad	Pepper Steak	Pan Seared Tuna	Avocado Pudding
20	Pasta Salad	Sicilian Seafood Stew	Beef Curry	Gingersnaps
21	Baked Apples With Cinnamon & Ginger	Sweet & Sour Ground Chicken	Rosemary Broiled Shrimp	Apple Crisp
22	Pear Banana Nut Muffins	Cuban Beef And Zucchini Kebabs	Vegetarian Pasta Bakes With Halloumi	Coconut Biscotti
23	Steel Cut Oatmeal	White Bean, Chicken, And Rosemary Casserole	Broccoli Pesto Penne With Chili And Garlic	Carob And Peanut Butter Balls
24	Corn Porridge With Maple And Raisins	Easy Turkey Meatloaf "Muffins"	Fritto Misto With Gremolata	Spiced Walnuts
25	English Muffins	Beef Massaman Curry	Barbecued Rump Of Beef In Dijon	Cinnamon Popcorn
26	Muesli-Style Oatmeal	Turkey With Greens	Grilled Chicken With Thyme	Baked Apples With Tahini Raisin Filling
27	Mexican Breakfast Toast	Pepper And Onion Tart	Marinated Lamb Steaks	Cheesecake Mousse With Raspberries
28	Milky Oat	Avocado Cream & Noodles	Oat And Chickpea Dumplings	Pumpkin Pudding Parfaits

CHAPTER 10:
FAQ

When is Surgery Required?

Suppose medication doesn't stop your acid reflux. In that case, prolonged exposure of the esophageal mucosa to the gastric acid may lead to severe complications of GERD, such as erosive esophagitis, Barrett's esophagus, esophageal stricture, aspiration pneumonia, and adenocarcinoma. Surgical treatment for GERD is recommended for treating chronic situations.

Surgery is a good option for prolonged medical therapy if you suffer from severe acid reflux symptoms. To treat severe and complicated acid reflux, it is advisable to opt for surgery because it offers better and faster results than medical therapy.

What are the Risks and Complications?

If you lack concern about the issue and delay treatment, it can lead to severe complications. They seem to be minor issues, but they can never be so reckless that you must face the critical music. Here are the difficulties you may have to face:

- The borderline of the esophagus can be damaged and inflamed, causing constant irritation, internal bleeding, and ulceration in some cases.
- Non-stop burning and internal irritation can affect overall health and enhance psychological pressure.
- There can be scar development that will lead to difficulty swallowing, and food will not be able to travel down the esophagus
- The repeated exposure of the cells and tissues to the stomach acid can change their formation. It can damage the cell structure, causing them to die and potentially develop cancer.

Focusing on the problem in the first stage is necessary to help with the proper treatment. In case of permanent negligence, things can be challenging to control and will come up with some ultimately damaging results as a whole.

What are Some Common Preventions?

The preventions of acid reflux are more related to your food options than hygienic conditions. It is a lifestyle problem that can occur and trigger your mismanagement of food, posture, habits, and lifestyle. Therefore, you must follow some safe lifestyle options to avoid further damage to your body.

Using the prevention options, you can avoid the factors that can cause acid reflux, such as heartburn, obesity, depression, drugs, hernia, and much more. In our body, everything is linked, so you have to ensure that your body is healthy overall. Remember, good health can help you have a good life and avoid all serious threats and issues.

What Role Does Nutrition Have in Preventing or Alleviating Acid Reflux?

It is possible that what, when, and how you eat will assist you in managing your symptoms. Eating smaller, more frequent meals throughout the day and avoiding food within three hours of bedtime seems beneficial for some people. Chewing thoroughly and eating in a calm and relaxed manner may also be helpful strategies, as may lowering the fat and carbohydrate quantity of your meal (particularly simple sugars).

It's important to remember that what causes your heartburn will be unique to you; therefore, depending on your journey of discovery, what helps you manage it will also be unique to you.

What Role Does My Way of Life Play in Helping or Hindering Acid Reflux?

If you smoke, are overweight, have high-stress levels, use certain medications such as non-steroidal anti-inflammatory drugs (NSAIDs) or anti-histamines, or are in the latter stages of pregnancy (usually from 27 weeks onwards), your symptoms may worsen. Always consult your doctor before making any big changes, especially before changing your medication regimen if you are on prescription medicine.

Making lifestyle changes is the primary line of treatment for the vast majority of people. When it comes to people who suffer from nighttime ailments, elevating the bedhead or employing a wedge-shaped pillow is one of the most helpful alterations. This is an easy victory for most people — strive to elevate your bedhead by 20-28cm to see results.

It is also possible to get benefits by avoiding wearing tight clothing, which is especially important for individuals who have excess belly obesity, and by refraining from lying down or bending immediately after eating. It's also a good idea not to work out right after a meal but rather to wait 1-2 hours for digestion to do its work.

CONCLUSION

Acid reflux is a stomach-related or digestive disorder that creates irritation and a restless condition for a person. The main reason behind this issue is poor digestion, improper food intake, lack of sleep, and inactivity. An increase in obesity and other health complications can cause acid reflux. In this chronic disorder, a person feels heartburn and feels like their food is not properly being digested. Stomach acid and food reverse into the food canal, which causes an inability to perform the task, and continuous burps can also affect a person's productivity. As per the consultants, it is necessary to treat acid reflux at the initial stage with food intake, exercise, and diet control by reducing weight or following proper medication. If it is not treated well, it may cause further health complications like cancer or ulcers.

To get quick relief from acid reflux, it is necessary to adopt certain dietary changes like taking small meals instead of full meals, following an exercise routine, reducing citrus intake, limiting spicy and fried food intake, and reducing weight.

At the initial stage of acid reflux, it can be treated and prevented with healthy and organic food choices. It also requires a proper medical checkup, which helps determine the severity of the problem. Consulting doctors and taking their advice on the treatment and precautions are necessary steps a person has to take to avoid gastric acid reflux. This book mentions several healthy and organic recipes that will help a person enjoy good food and relieve acid reflux conditions.

Printed in Great Britain
by Amazon

13826438R00088